Life Coaching
A Manual for Helping Professionals

Dave Ellis

With special thanks to

JoAnne Bangs
Stan Lankowitz
and
Bill Rentz

Crown House Publishing Limited
www.crownhouse.co.uk

Published by
Crown House Publishing Ltd
Crown Buildings
Bancyfelin, Carmarthen, Wales, SA33 5ND, UK
www.crownhouse.co.uk
and
Crown House Publishing Company, LLC
6 Trowbrdige Drive, Ste. 5, Bethel, CT 06801
www.crownhousepublishing.com

British Library Catalouging-in-Publications Data
A catalog entry for this book is available
from the British Library.

13 digit ISBN: 978-190442494-9
10 digit ISBN: 1904424945

LCCN 2005937426

Printed in the United States of America

For my parents, Ken and Maryellen Ellis, who gave me one piece of advice, which was not to give advice. From their instruction and example, I discovered that assisting others to create a wonderful life usually involves more listening than advising.

People do not have to become something they are not. They need to learn only who and what they really are.

EKNATH EASWARAN

Go to the people, live with them, love them, learn from them, work with them, start from what they have, build on what they know, and in the end, when the work is done, the people will rejoice and say: We have done it ourselves.

LAO TZU

Preface

This book is written for currently practicing professional life coaches and for people who intend to enter this profession. Of course, this book alone is not sufficient preparation to become a life coach. *Life Coaching* is a comprehensive manual for assisting someone who is already trained as a helping professional (such as a counselor, social worker, minister) to begin a career as a life coach.

There has been a flood of news articles and books written about life coaching in the last few years. And there are a variety of places where life coaches can receive training. As with many new professions, there is little agreement about what life coaching really is. In this book, I do not intend to review the ideas of others or to reach a consensus regarding the nature of this profession. Instead, I present a model of what I believe works in assisting people to create the life of their dreams.

This model is based on work that I have done over the last 25 years with college students, college faculty and administrators, and professionals involved mostly in non-profit organizations. This model is described in detail in my other books and is particularly well presented in the book *Falling Awake*. *Falling Awake* and the accompanying workshops, video and audio programs, and website are companion materials for *Life Coaching*. Clients of the coaches who use our style of coaching can also use this material. *Falling Awake* is like a textbook and is designed for use by clients who are receiving life coaching.

My definition of life coaching differs from the way that many people understand this term. I almost wish I had a different word for this way of being with people, since I often hear the word *coaching* used in a way that I would never use it. Many people think they are coaching when they say: "Let me give you some advice," "I can consult with you," or, "I can teach you some skills to solve that problem."

There's nothing wrong with a vision of coaching that includes consultation, teaching, and advice, but what I mean by coaching is something entirely different. *In life coaching, my aim is to assist people to create their own solutions, arrive at their own answers, and discover options for themselves.* When we promote this kind of creativity in our clients, they're far more likely to bring the results of life coaching into their daily lives and produce lasting change.

Others who write about or teach life coaching may therefore read what I've written here and say that it does not represent what they mean by life coaching. With respect, I say, "I know, but it is what *I* mean by life coaching. I don't present this material as an argument for a point of view but rather as a possibility for how we can help others to discover their passions and unlock their brilliance."

A note about gender-fair language
In order to be gender-inclusive while avoiding awkward sentence constructions, I chose to alternate the use of male and female pronouns throughout this book.

More about Falling Awake

Falling Awake: Creating the Life of Your Dreams is an interactive book that assists life coaching clients to identify what they want in all areas of their life for the rest of their lives and to develop ways to achieve those dreams. This book is often the "textbook" that can provide the teaching that most life coaches do not have time to do during their sessions. It covers a wide range of life skills from stress management to communications to long range planning.

In addition to the *Falling Awake* book, this material is also presented for life coaching clients in workshops, video and audio programs, and a comprehensive website. The website provides for free: 1) a Wake-Up Call™ service, 2) a life-planning program, 3) data-based journaling, and 4) a downloadable version of *Falling Awake*. You can find out more about all of these services and a schedule of upcoming workshops by visiting www.FallingAwake.com or by writing to:

Falling Awake
P.O. Box 8396
Rapid City, SD 57709
USA

Acknowledgments

Stan Lankowitz was one of the first people I used as a life coach, and he soon became my best friend. He now works as a full-time life coach. Stan edited this book in a way that was more cowriting than editing. I appreciate all that I have gained from him as a friend, coauthor, and coach.

JoAnne Bangs, Richard Kiefer, and Bill Rentz have been assisting me in the last many years to teach our particular style of life coaching to beginning and experienced life coaches. Through our work together they have taught me much about how we can assist others to have a great life.

I also thank Doug Toft who is an amazing writer and editor. He has been wonderful at helping me express in writing what I generally present verbally. I thank him for being such a joyful coworker and coauthor.

Thanks also to the many people who have been my life coaches over the last 25 years. I am amazed at how much they have contributed to my life by saying so very little but saying it so very powerfully. I also thank the people who have let me be their life coach. It is through this practice that most of the ideas in this book were developed.

The people who have participated in the workshops I have given over the last 25 years have taught me a great deal about trusting the genius in each of us. I also thank the people who participated in the life coaching schools I have conducted. They have added dozens of ideas to this book.

One of the most wonderful things about my life is that I get to work with a group of people that I deeply love and admire. It is this community that gives birth to my work. In addition to those

I have already mentioned, I also want to acknowledge Duane Elgin, Robbie Murchison, Doane Robinson, and Leonard Running.

Any list of acknowledgements regarding my work would be incomplete without celebrating the wonderful support and partnership of my wife, Trisha Waldron, and my daughters, who continually support me to reach the life of my dreams.

Request for feedback

Having written several books that have gone into multiple editions, I know that a book is never complete after only one edition. One of the books I authored is now in its eleventh edition and has improved with each rewrite because of the input of thousands of people. Please help me with the next edition of this book by letting me know what you think of it. Send your ideas, suggestions, complaints, and compliments to:

Dave Ellis
Breakthrough Enterprises, Inc.
P.O. Box 8396
Rapid City, SD 57709
USA

Contents

Preface..v

More about *Falling Awake* vi

Acknowledgments ix

Request for feedback x

Chapter One   The Power and Possibility of Life Coaching 1

Discovering passion, unlocking brilliance *1*
Life coaches usually meet with clients many hours a
month over several years. Through coaching, clients
can achieve the life of their dreams by discovering
their passions and uncovering their genius.

Major benefits of life coaching *4*
Our clients can gain benefits such as a larger vision,
inspired creativity, expanded possibilities, someone
who listens fully, unconditional acceptance, focused
attention beyond sessions, access to the domain of
being, and our full commitment.

Key qualities of life coaches.....................................*10*
Effective life coaches often display joyful service,
passion for personal development, ability to see
genius in people, and willingness to coach from a
blank canvas.

Life coaching as a distinct career *19*
Life coaching differs in key ways from both
counseling and consulting.

Chapter Two   Mechanics of Life Coaching *23*

Choosing times and ways to meet *23*
A coaching session can last anywhere from five
minutes to several days and take place through
almost any medium.

Creating and using a life coaching agreement 26
Use written agreements to spell out what
clients can expect of you—and what you ask
of clients.

Getting started with a client..28
Ask what the client wants, summarize the
mechanics of coaching, survey the client's life, ask
for conflicts between values and behavior, and ask
for complaints and celebrations. Also listen a lot
and go longer than usual.

Preparing for sessions...32
Renew your commitment to the client, review
your notes, set an agenda while being willing
to scrap it, and get into the "zone" for life
coaching.

Staying focused during sessions...36
Commit to be present, pay attention to your
attention, ask clients to repeat themselves,
write distraction cards, write action plans,
report distractions, and consider scheduling
another time.

Taking notes...39
Take notes consciously, present your notes to your
client, and occasionally feed back the client's exact
words.

Completing sessions...41
Consider giving assignments and writing letters to
clients.

Ending the life coaching relationship 43
Remember that you don't need any one client,
refer the client, ask for appreciations and
reflections, create a ceremony, begin another
kind of relationship, and assist the client to
move into the future.

Chapter Three　**The Coaching Continuum**.. **47**

The continuum—an overview *47*
The continuum ranges from the least directive
techniques to the most directive techniques.

The continuum in detail *48*
Listen fully and affirm. Listen fully and feed back
celebrations, dreams, and actions. Ask the client to
generate a few new possibilities. Ask the client to
generate many possibilities. Add to the client's list
of possibilities. Present at least ten possibilities
(some contradictory). Present at least three
possibilities. Teach a new technique. Offer an
option. Cautiously consider non-coaching
techniques, including giving advice.

Choose your place on the continuum.....................................*65*
Consciously choose where you want to be on the
continuum at any given moment and assist your
client in creating multiple action plans.

Chapter Four　**Enhancing Your Coaching Skills** **69**

Assisting clients to discover their passion *69*
Presume that clients are passionate, listen fully and
affirm, feed back their passion, open up an inquiry,
focus on being, create scenarios, and write down
what clients say. Also, ask clients to write, suspend
your judgment, ask for complaints, review the past,
and invite emotional discharge.

Knowing your client *77*
Become more familiar with your client by having
them draw a relationship map and by asking them
to review their life in five-year increments.

Evaluating your life coaching *78*
Monitor in the moment and evaluate afterwards,
review your session with colleagues, tape your
sessions, notice verbal and non-verbal cues, and use
verbal and written evaluations.

Using six types of conversation..84
Choose from sharing, debriefing, clearing,
discussion and debate, teaching, and coaching.

*Maintaining appropriate balance in the life
coaching relationship* 90
Share, carefully offer examples from your own life,
speak about yourself in a contributing way, and
nurture yourself.

Asking questions cautiously 92
Stop asking questions, substitute statements for
questions, and find alternatives to asking "why?".

Developing creativity and intuition 95
Assign your intuition a place, imagine what clients
are thinking, put yourself on the spot, admit that
you're stumped and then feed back the problem.

Creating ceremonies and rituals 98
Set aside time to celebrate what's working in the
client's life and mark important life changes.

Responding when clients don't follow through 100
Assist; don't insist. Hold goals lightly—and as
sacred commitments. Stop life coaching in certain
areas, and consider when to end the life coaching
relationship.

Responding when clients seem defensive.............................102
Release or downplay your interpretations and
judgments.

Assisting clients to be more self-responsible 105
Listen fully and affirm, offer alternatives to the
language of obligation, break large goals into
smaller steps, and assist clients to create many
options.

Coaching two people at once 108
Assume that people are committed to each other,
build rapport, and define and celebrate your role.
Assist people to share the conversation space, make
everyone "right," ask clients to speak what they've
withheld, and use the empty chair technique.

Coaching clients when you don't know or don't have it handled *113*
Admit you don't know, focus on process, distinguish coaching from consulting, remember the benefits of ignorance, and learn the subject.

Bringing your specialty carefully *115*
Avoid applying your specialty too widely. Be willing to explore all aspects of a client's life.

Acknowledging mistakes that life coaches make *116*
Mistakes include imposing values, judging clients, hiding mistakes, talking too much, leading the show, and thinking that we always know what the mistakes are.

Chapter Five   **Possible Topics to Teach** **119**

Get the most from life coaching *119*
Encourage clients to clear their slate for life coaching sessions, raise the stakes, communicate fully, own the coaching, summarize their discoveries and intentions, and speak their dreams.

Creating the future *122*
Assist clients to overcome possible obstacles to setting long-range, comprehensive goals. Also, present specific techniques, such as balancing conversation space and using two-week planning.

Solving problems *134*
Focus on solutions and choose from several models of problem-solving.

Changing habits *136*
Clients can learn to see most of their behavior as habits and apply a three-step method for changing any habit: commit to change, set up a feedback system, and practice without reproach.

Handling emotions *140*
Help clients discharge emotions and distinguish attachment from pleasure.

Speaking with self-responsibility..*146*
You can describe five elements of I-messages as a
way for clients to be self-generative in their
speaking.

Improving relationships...*149*
Clients can learn to recreate their experience of
other people and gain more skill at receiving
compliments.

Using success strategies *153*
Clients can use a core set of strategies to meet
almost any goal or produce nearly any result.

Chapter Six   **Professional Issues for Life Coaches............................ 159**

Developing appropriate intimacy with clients *159*
Avoid being too intimate—and too aloof. Ask for
permission to be candid, assume a certain level of
intimacy, and respond responsibly to sexual
attraction.

Handling dual relationships *163*
Recognize dual relationships, acknowledge the
danger, ensure a demand for coaching, limit the
coaching, clearly define your role in the moment,
release your agenda, and review your clients.

Making referrals to other professionals *166*
Consider your range of knowledge and skill. Refer
in cases of serious illness, when clients stop making
healthy choices, or when the problem reaches a
certain level. Negotiate for a psychological
assessment and choose when to coach people who
take psychiatric medications. Choose your place on
the referral continuum.

Responding to illegal or unethical activity...........................*171*
Know the applicable laws and declare up front
what you will keep confidential.

Continuing professional development *174*
Get mentoring about your coaching, take breaks,
and consider hiring your own life coach.

Chapter Seven   **Marketing Your Services** **177**

Three approaches to marketing 177
Clarity: Be clear about the value you provide.
Communication: Market by word of mouth. Media:
Choose whether to use promotional materials.

Leaving a verbal calling card 180
Practice briefly describing your service.

Attracting clients you love to coach 182
Let clients self-select and consider many types of
clients. Approach people with big goals. State your
qualifications, meet other life coaches, and offer
your service to organizations. Be prepared to
answer objections.

Making the transition to self-employment 187
Set goals, make the transition gradually, and find
partners. Set aside working hours, a physical space,
and even clothes. Also set your fees.

Chapter Eight   **Questions and Answers About Life Coaching**........... **193**

Questions about life coaching as a career 193
Is life coaching an elitist field? Could I coach
someone who has other life coaches? Do I need to
know people before approaching them as clients?

*Questions about coaching people who seem
"stuck"* 195
How can I respond when clients keep cancelling
sessions? How can I help clients move past
resignation? How can I assist clients to choose from
a variety of options?

Questions about staying effective as a life coach 197
Who am I to be a life coach, anyway? How can I
coach people when my own life is not working that
well? Is it useful for me to meet with a client's
relatives, co-workers, or friends? Is it ever useful to
behave outrageously on purpose? How do I stay
grounded in process and avoid getting lost in
content? How do I live up to a great first session?

Bring your own questions and answers 201
You can invent questions leading to your own
answers that will dramatically improve your ability
to coach people.

Bibliography..205
About the author 207
Life coach training—a 15-month curriculum 207

Index..209

Chapter One
The Power and Possibility of Life Coaching

Discovering passion, unlocking brilliance

The purpose of this book is to describe a specific type of life coaching called, "Life Coaching from Falling Awake." In general, life coaching is a process whereby the coach assists the client to improve the quality of his or her life. Of course, this is a purpose similar to what people receive through counseling, consulting, teaching, ministry, and friendship. The difference is that life coaching provides this partnership without any agenda other than the client's. This career is relatively new.

In 1996, I set a goal that by the year 2006 there would be 10,000 practicing life coaches. At the time, I thought that was doable but unlikely. Now, it looks like a reality. I also had a goal that by 2001 many people would want life coaching as much as they want a house. I've met a few people for whom that is also a reality. For me, having this kind of a partner—someone who is totally committed to helping me achieve what I want in all areas of my life—makes a huge difference. If necessary, I'd give up my house, rent an apartment, or even live in a tent so that I could hire a life coach.

Life coaches assist people to discover what a great life they already have, what they want in every area of their lives for the rest of their lives, and ways to unlock their own brilliance to achieve their dreams. To do that, life coaches usually meet with clients many hours a month over several years, assisting them to achieve the life of their dreams by discovering their passions and uncovering their genius.

By meeting with a life coach, people can create and achieve goals in every area of life. This happens through frequent contact with a life coach who serves as the clients' full partner in their personal transformation.

Life coaching is not just a collection of techniques—it's a form of relationship that's both confidential and life changing. People usually reveal more to their life coach than to their friends, counselors, or even to their spouse. Through this relationship, clients can move quickly from problems to solutions, from insight to action, from the status quo to completely new outcomes in their lives.

Life coaches provide a service for people who are already happy and successful. Basically, life coaching clients have got life "handled." As a life coach, I am committed to bring these people to that deep, soulful sense that they are free—free from their obligations, their limitations, their fears, and any other obstacles to realize their full passion and brilliance. I don't know of a greater gift that we can bring to people.

Our clients can quickly create the life of their dreams

I think it's possible to learn to be with people in such a way that their lives transform *quickly*. By the word quickly, I don't mean in a few days, but I do mean in a few weeks, a few months, and absolutely within a few years. What I offer in this book are ways that you and I can be this way with more people, more consistently.

We succeed as life coaches when our clients feel empowered and valuable—confident, secure, and filled with new options. When clients leave their sessions with a renewed burst of energy, then we know the coaching is working. And when we're skilled in the art of life coaching, clients can experience this in a five-minute interaction as well as in a five-hour session.

You can dramatically improve your ability to be with people, such that in a few months they can authentically report that they won the lottery of life. As a life coach, you can assist people in a short time to authentically say, "Today, I'm living the life of my dreams."

Life coaches trade in miracles

It is miraculous to me what people can create when given the opportunity to solve their own problems without advice—when given the possibility and support to create the life of their choosing.

Life coaching is an amazing career. I don't see any profession that does more for people. For over 25 years, I've coached people and I've received life coaching. From the conversations I've had with my coaches, I've dramatically shifted my daily activities. I've changed how much I delegate, how much I work, how much I spend, how I take care of my health, how I relate to my wife, how much pleasure I experience, how I contribute to people, and much more.

I believe that anyone who receives life coaching can experience this same level of transformation. People can have a wonderful life almost instantly no matter what their circumstances—no matter the state of their health or their finances, their home or their relationships. With a life coach, they can overcome almost any obstacle to a wonderful life. Clients can leave a life coaching session with dozens of viable options for getting past obstacles—including many options that are wildly creative.

Life coaches are unbiased partners who support their clients' agendas and keep bringing them back to a conversation of 1) celebration, 2) dreams (what they passionately desire), and 3) actions (ways they can fulfill their desires). You and I can be life coaches—people with the rare and precious job of keeping that conversation alive.

As much as anything else you bring to a life coaching relationship, you bring the miraculous possibility that your clients can become totally alive. This is a way of being that people very seldom experience. Think about the number of people you meet who regularly enjoy deep intimacy, vibrant health, full celebration, and daily ecstasy. As a life coach, this is what you help clients create. In doing that, you are probably giving as much as one person can give another.

Please let in my enthusiasm about life coaching. On every page of this book, I want to communicate how enamored I am with this new career and how much it benefits people. Opening up to the power and possibility of this new profession can propel you toward full effectiveness as a life coach.

Major benefits of life coaching

Life coaches create value by assisting clients to solve problems. But if that's all that we do, then our clients continually need problems in order to keep working with us.

Efficient problem-solving is only part of the power and possibility of life coaching. When we coach from a larger context, we can bring all of the following benefits as well.

Constant celebration

Life coaches promote celebration and a deep appreciation of life. We encourage our clients to truly see how fortunate they are in every area of life.

Many people go through their life not realizing how wealthy they are in comparison to all of the other people on the planet. Most people don't appreciate how healthy and loved they are. One of the jobs of a life coach is to help our clients wake up to what a great life they have.

A larger vision

Life coaches can bring a vision of people that goes beyond their vision of themselves. When we see others as bigger than they see themselves to be, we empower them. We imagine our clients experiencing profound shifts in their lives and generating projects that will outlast them for many lifetimes. We listen to our clients and take their dreams seriously in a way that no one ever has before.

You and I have the potential to be with people in such a way that their lives are altered forever. When we go beyond what they *have* and *do* to who they *are*, clients can see themselves as creative, intelligent, loving, and generous. That's really how I see my clients, and I don't have to make it up. I ask you to bring this attitude to everyone you coach. And if it happens that you don't see someone this way, then do whatever you need to do so that you can—or get him a different coach.

Inspired creativity

A life coach consistently listens, speaks, and occasionally asks questions in a way that draws forth his client's genius and creativity. For any given problem, clients can generate a long list of great solutions. Often this happens when the life coach simply brings full listening and full commitment to the interaction and just invites people to stay in the inquiry: "Well, what could you do about this problem? Okay, now what else might you do?"

Sometimes life coaching seems like a think tank where clients are constantly creating and inventing new options. Life coaching is about people generating their own answers, not looking outside of themselves for solutions. This process is not about teaching what you already know or about clients acting as students. Instead, life coaching is empowering people to invent something new—to think something they've never thought before and to say something they've never said before.

Expanded possibilities

Our clients can expand their sense of what's possible to be, do, and have during their lifetimes. If people who enter life coaching have a common denominator, it's probably a spark of realization that life can be ten times better than it is now, even if life is currently great.

Part of my job as a coach is to bring forth possibilities that aren't immediately obvious to people, no matter what arena of life we're discussing.

A potential client might say, "What I really want from working with a coach is a life that's free of debt."

"Great," I'll reply. "Yes, you can get out of debt. And, if you want, you can take on the goal of having two years' worth of your salary in savings. You could even manage your money so well that you're able to give away 20 percent of your income every month. Those are just a couple of possibilities available to you in addition to getting debt-free."

What I'm doing here is creating new possibilities for people—not telling them what to do. I don't say, "You know what you *should* do? You really should put two-years' worth of money in the bank and then give away 20 percent of your income." I think that "shoulding" on people disempowers them. My goal is to open up new possibilities.

In my experience, people do not hold the possibility that they can create a life filled with joy, intimacy, pleasure, health, and financial well being. Some people even feel guilty about the prospect of having a life that grand. We as life coaches can be the voice for a wonderful life. We can just keep bringing this conversation about possibilities to clients—a conversation that they seldom get anywhere else.

Someone who listens fully

In addition to bringing a larger vision, inspired creativity, and an expanded sense of possibility, we create tremendous value just by listening fully and deeply. This is something that few people experience in any of their relationships.

Full listening happens when we allow people to survey all areas of their lives and speak with total candor about what works and what doesn't. Full listening happens when we allow clients to share, to celebrate successes, to cry, to grieve, and to laugh—all without fear of judgment.

Another way we listen fully is by releasing all of our personal agendas. Life coaching is assisting people with their agenda on their terms. If a client is clear that picking weeds in her garden or crying for an hour is the best use of our time together, then that's what we can do.

We give people something they probably get nowhere else—a partner that has no agenda except theirs. What a huge and rare contribution to bring to people!

Unconditional acceptance

Life coaches can offer unconditional love. In my experience, this type of relationship is rare. If we provided only this, we would be bringing enough to help people create miracles. And we can provide much more.

Loving unconditionally means that in each interaction with a client we are gentle, non-antagonistic, and non-confrontational—no shame, no blame. Relating to people with an "in-your-face," confrontational approach can sometimes work, but I do not recommend that this take place in coaching. My goal is that life coaches don't "get on a client's case"—and that clients don't get on their own cases. When people are made to feel "wrong," or make themselves wrong, they often stop setting goals, especially big goals, and that's contrary to my vision of life coaching.

Some clients might ask you to "get on their case" or to "hold them accountable" in order to help them keep a promise, change a habit, or move forward in their life. I usually tell people that I won't do this. What I can do is remind them of their promises and goals without blaming them for not doing what they have said they would do.

Focused attention beyond sessions

Between coaching sessions, your clients can still be in your thoughts. I tell clients that one of the benefits of having me as a life coach is that I'll spend time every day thinking about them: "I will hold you in my consciousness more than anyone else does, except possibly your mother or your father. I will review your goals and dreams and think about your struggles. I'm there for you constantly. That's how much of a partner I am for you."

Often I request photographs of my clients. That way I can look at an image of each person every morning, remember my commitment to their success, and bring their visions, dreams, and goals into my heart.

When I hear these things from a life coach, I feel valued in a way that's absolutely unique. Even when I am not in contact with my own life coaches, I still know that there are people who are rooting for me—people who are completely committed to my agenda and who care for me unconditionally.

Change in all domains

Clients can create the life of their dreams in three domains: *having*, *doing*, and *being*.

Many people are out of balance because they focus primarily on what they have—their jobs, their money, their cars, their houses, and their relationships. These people often act as if they are human "havings"—as if the only thing they need to do to be happy is to rearrange their circumstances.

Others can become "human doings." They can be dominated by what they do—the work they do, the community service they do, the trips that they take, and the exercise they do.

I am not saying that there's something wrong with having or doing. I am saying that people often minimize or forget about another domain—the domain of being. When we coach in this domain, we assist clients to define the core values and fundamental commitments that constantly shape what they choose to do and have. As life coaches, we can keep bringing clients back to a conversation about who they are, beyond their actions and circumstances. We can bring the domain of being to lives dominated by doing and having.

My goal is to achieve balance and help clients get what they want in all three of these domains. I want them to live effectively in the domain of being—to make moment-to-moment choices based on their deepest values. I also want them to be able to do most everything they've ever dreamed of doing and to have the circumstances of their dreams.

While keeping balance among these three domains in mind, I will bend over backwards in assisting people to achieve the life of their dreams in *any* one of these domains. As a life coach, I resist the temptation to steer clients away from "materialistic" goals in the domain of having and guide them toward goals that are more doing- or being-oriented. If a client comes to me and says, "What I want is an expensive house and a fancy car," then I'll say, "Great, I can help you have those things."

Benefits to people beyond the client

In 1995, Stan Lankowitz and I completed a book titled *Human Being: A Manual for Happiness, Health, Love, and Wealth.* When we conceived this book, our aim was to communicate ideas in a way that would dramatically alter the quality of each reader's life. What's more, we wanted *Human Being* to have a similar effect on people who knew the reader—even if these people didn't read the book.

As life coaches, we can adopt a similar goal. When our clients bring more happiness, health, love, and wealth to themselves, they benefit their coworkers, friends, and families as well as their organizations and communities. This fact reinforces the usefulness of multi-year and even multi-decade relationships with our clients. When we partner with people over the long-term, we help them win the lottery of life *and* create value for the people and projects they love.

Freedom from suffering and self-discipline

I often meet people who subscribe to the philosophy of "no pain, no gain." Even though people can create value from their suffering and self-discipline, this is not the path that I recommend to my clients. I want people to live out their visions, dreams, and goals with a minimum of pain, struggle, upset, and turmoil.

Suffering and self-discipline are not always necessary to personal growth and development. Through life coaching, clients can get to the life of their dreams while staying lighthearted and taking actions that seem almost effortless.

Full commitment

Tremendous progress can be generated simply out of our commitment to clients. This is 90 percent of what life coaching is about—being completely committed to the client's agenda in life. This commitment gives people power.

You don't need lots of techniques or years of experience to be an effective life coach. What contributes to people most is your level of commitment to them. That commitment doesn't come from technique or experience—it comes from the depths of your being.

Key qualities of life coaches

Life coaches are committed to joyful service

Service without joy can too easily turn into resentment and, rather than being a gift, can become a burden for both the giver and receiver. As life coaches, we experience joy when we serve others and consider it an honor. We are committed to leaving people in better shape than we found them and are thrilled when given the opportunity to assist clients to get what they want in their lives.

In order to serve clients effectively, we suspend our own thoughts about what's most important and, instead, commit solely to our client's purpose and agenda.

As a life coach, I enjoy knowing specifically how I can serve my client. To find out how I can be most empowering from moment to moment, I can look to my client for direction. I could ask, "Do you still want to talk about money issues today, as we'd planned, or is there something else that is more important to you right now?" Or I could ask, "Would you like me to just listen or would you prefer that I facilitate some problem-solving?"

Life coaches have confidence in clients

Life coaches facilitate miracles in people's lives. This can be a daunting and even frightening challenge if we think we have to do this all by ourselves. But we don't. We know that our clients are brilliant, loving, and generous partners in the process. We trust that our clients can quickly and permanently create wonderful lives.

Life coaches do more than listen *to* people—we listen *for* people. We listen for what might be dormant or hidden. We listen for evidence of positive qualities that our clients might not have distinguished in themselves. We listen *for* people's magnificence. We listen *for* the greatness in who people are becoming.

When life coaches listen for people in this way, these positive qualities rise to the surface and manifest more frequently and more powerfully. The way life coaches interact with clients is a contribution that helps clients know in the depths of their souls that they are geniuses.

Even when a client is feeling low on confidence and is self-deprecating, a life coach can stand in contradiction to the client's current mood or point of view. While having empathy and complete understanding, a life coach knows that a foundation of brilliance and competence lies just beneath their client's negative self-esteem.

Now, I can't prove that you, I, and our clients are all geniuses. I don't have your IQ scores and I don't have your clients' IQ scores. But I just know in my heart that the people I interact with are geniuses. When I trust that of myself and of them, then what we create during a coaching conversation rises to the level of genius.

11

One of the most powerful tools I use in my coaching is to communicate this promise to each of my clients: "I will interact with you knowing that you are brilliant, capable, loving, contributing, resourceful, generous, and creative. And if you ever appear differently than this, I'll know that I've just made an error and that I'm not seeing you as you really are."

In addition to having confidence in our clients, we as life coaches also trust the desires of our clients. We are confident that clients know what is best for themselves. We believe that when clients follow their own authentic desires, they end up promoting the highest good for the largest number of people.

Even if a client follows a well-examined desire and it gets the client into some kind of trouble, coaches trust that the consequences of the client's actions and what is learned as a result of that action is an effective way to move the client forward. Of course, if the client is planning some illegal, unethical, or immoral activity, I do my best to stop it.

Life coaches trust what their clients say. Even when their words seem to conflict with some of their behaviors, life coaches still trust what their clients say. If, for example, a client says that he wants to lose weight and yet does not exercise and maintains the same poor eating habits, a life coach knows that the behaviors are just a bunch of habits that have not yet changed to be consistent with the client's stated goal. The behaviors in no way dilute the integrity of the client's words that he truly wants to lose weight.

Life coaches trust the process

Life coaches know that life coaching works. We are very certain that clients can use life coaching to create miracles in their lives. This clarity is not theoretical. It is gained through their own direct experience and through the reports of others. This belief is contagious when we have an unshakable belief in the value of life coaching. The more confidence clients have in the process, the more effectively they will be able to use it to create more of whatever they want in their lives.

Life coaches are accountable

We are not only trusting, we are also trustworthy. We keep appointments, we keep whatever agreements we make, and we keep confidences. As life coaches, when we make mistakes and do not keep our word, we report the mistake, do what we can to repair any damages, and assure our clients that we remain committed to keeping our word and being accountable.

In many settings and relationships in the world, when a promise is not kept, it's no big deal. In these cases, keeping promises is not valued very highly. Coaches set a different standard. We have different expectations and model the power of keeping promises. Life coaches know that when a promise is made, words float out into the universe bearing a vision of what is to come. When actions are aligned with those words, intentions become realities. This is a process that clients can use to create the life of their dreams.

Life coaches are passionate about personal and professional growth

Life coaches are passionate about ongoing personal and professional development. This is a big part of why I coach people. I want to constantly learn, grow, and improve. I want to be more effective both as a life coach and as a human being who enjoys high levels of health, happiness, love, and wealth in my own life. Life coaching keeps me in conversations about personal and professional effectiveness and helps me make continual progress toward achieving my goals.

Life coaches are neither stuck nor positioned. We are open to change, willing to take risk, and comfortable trying on different points of view. We are constantly looking for ways to improve.

Life coaches are not too proud to ask for and receive help. Many coaches are so very clear about the benefits of coaching that they have their own coaches. I certainly do. Actually, I have several coaches, and I use them all the time.

Even though coaches have challenges and ups and downs just like everyone else, we are knowledgeable about a wide variety of success strategies and are practiced at using them. They are generally living balanced, fulfilling, joyful, and contributing lives.

Life coaches are life-long learners. We are able to offer many current personal examples, refer to a wide variety of literature, and bring relevant, accurate information to our conversations. We use what we've learned to inject useful analogies and metaphors whenever appropriate.

Life coaches establish rapport

A relationship with a life coach is one of the most personal and intimate relationships that a person can have. When conversations are safe, when listening is effective, and when strong rapport has been developed, clients are willing to reveal their deepest desires and most troublesome concerns.

One of the most effective ways to establish rapport is to use the first strategy on the coaching continuum, which is to listen fully and affirm. Fully understanding and accepting clients' thoughts, emotions, and actions strengthen the bond that holds relationships together.

Life coaches think creatively

When life coaches are adding to clients' lists of possibilities or presenting their own, the ability to think creatively can help clients break out of old paradigms and create new interpretations that are more empowering. Generating many different (and even contradictory) ideas, options, solutions, and menus can give clients a greater sense of freedom.

When holding up a mirror, life coaches use our creative thinking to polish up and enhance whatever the client has spoken before sending it back.

Life coaches think creatively to accommodate special preferences and unique needs of our clients. We can invent a wide variety of options regarding times of sessions, duration of sessions, places to meet, methods of communication, styles of feedback, menus of topics, and just about anything else related to the structure and dynamics of coaching our clients.

Life coaches think critically

Life coaches assist clients to apply critical thinking skills to achieve goals. We also understand that critical thinking is just one helpful tool, and that other tools, such as intuition and emotions, can access powerful domains of intelligence and wisdom.

There are numerous ways that life coaches can effectively use critical thinking. Here are just a few:

- The ability to categorize and prioritize can turn a loosely formulated and random set of ideas into a thoughtful, meaningful, strategically organized life plan.
- Assisting clients to distinguish between fact and opinion can open up possibilities of new paradigms and interpretations that result in happier, more fulfilling lives.
- Using critical thinking to challenge even the most cherished convictions can lead to more freedom.
- Critical thinking skills can assist clients to untangle complex situations so that they can think more clearly about them and develop action plans more appropriate to the various elements of the problem or goal.
- By comparing their behaviors with their values, clients can be less influenced by the immediate pushes, pulls, desires, and aversions of their circumstances and make choices more consistent with who they intend to be.
- Life coaches can help clients gain clarity about something by gently suggesting that clients consider the possibility that they are making some of the more common errors in thinking such as using double standards, stereotyping, and accepting unsubstantiated assumptions.

Life coaches facilitate powerful processes

As life coaches, we have a variety of processes in our toolboxes to assist clients in resolving current problems, exploring new possibilities, designing effective and powerful action plans, creating visions for the future that are clear, compelling and wonderful, and living the life of their dreams.

These processes include facilitating emotional release, promoting promises and commitment, inventing powerful interpretations, and creating multiple solutions and pathways to achieve any goal. Processes that life coaches use are content free and can be applied to many different issues, circumstances, and goals.

Life coaches pay attention to language

The way clients speak and their choice of words reveal attitudes, values, beliefs, and intentions that are fairly good predictors of outcomes, both successful and unsuccessful. Client language offers clues than invite strategies that promote progress.

In my book, *Falling Awake,* I talk about the ladder of powerful speaking. The main purpose of this approach is to offer a way for people to use their language to move from being victims to being more self-responsible. When clients use words like "I should," "I have to," "I must," or "They made me," they are giving their power away to others and are playing the role of victims. When clients use other words like, "I could," "I'd prefer to," "I'd love to," "I plan to," and "I promise," they are moving closer to being responsible and taking effective action. Life coaches can discuss this use of language with clients and assist them to be in more control of their lives.

You can read the article about the ladder of powerful speaking for free by visiting my website www.fallingawake.com and clicking on "Get the Book Free" and then on "Table of Contents." In the chapter "Success Strategy #4 – Take Responsibility", the article is titled "Escaping victim mud." In fact, you can read any article in the entire book for free at this website.

The article immediately following "Escaping victim mud" is titled "Speak from 'I'." It offers a way to use the less threatening language in "I" messages instead of the more blaming language in "you" messages. Listening for and discussing this distinction is another way to empower clients.

Another example of the benefits of paying close attention to language is that life coaches can help their clients turn complaints into requests. For example, "We never have any fun anymore" can be heard as "Can we plan to go for a hike or do something that's fun next weekend?"

Life coaches can also translate complaints they receive from their clients into requests that lead to positive changes. "I have a problem because I really want to talk with you next week but I'll be on a cruise ship in the Caribbean" can be heard as "I'll be on a cruise ship in the Caribbean next week and would you help me find a way to talk with you?"

Life coaches coach from a blank canvas

Great life coaches come to a session with a carefully prepared agenda and then completely release that agenda.

Before I see clients or talk to them over the telephone, I mentally review their life and their commitments. And then I review my notes where I have kept track of the highlights of their lives and the topics we discussed in our last several meetings. From this, I create an agenda that reflects what I think the client wants and what she might have said that she would like to do during this meeting.

Setting this agenda prepares me to be of the most service. Then, I throw the agenda away.

Michel Renaud, a life coach in Montreal, once asked the painter Peter Max how he could be so productive as an artist. "The discipline I have is to just walk into the studio and be in front of the canvas with no agenda," Max said. With a background in meditation, Max can completely let go of everything on his mind. He creates a space inside himself resembling a blank canvas, staying present moment-to-moment with nothing predetermined. Then he just paints one stroke after another and an amazing work of art shows up.

Renaud says his intention is to do the same thing when coaching people: "I create a space for that person to discover what they have to discover and then be pertinent to that moment. Meeting Peter Max showed me that my job is to bring emptiness and a blank space instead of all my history and baggage with the client."

Coming to this blank space can be hard when we bring assumptions about the differences between people. For example, I could assume that there's a huge difference between coaching men and coaching women. I could also assume there is a big difference between coaching someone who is 20 years old and someone who is 40. And, I could assume that coaching someone who grew up in a rural area is different than coaching someone who grew up in a large city.

The trick is to acknowledge all those differences and go beyond them. I don't like to assume that people's gender, income level, race, or age explains who they are or why they do what they do. I think that categorizing people and then coming up with ways to coach them based on those categories is a mistake. I want to coach to the soul, not to the category—male versus female, black versus white, gay versus straight, old versus young.

I do not want to depend on any preconceptions about the differences between people when I coach them. While coaching, I want to continually return to the blank canvas that Peter Max and Michel Renaud talk about. I want to release any thoughts such as, "When I'm with men, I'm going to coach them one way, and when I'm with women, I'm going to coach them a different way." My commitment is to let go of such thoughts and approach each human being with a blank canvas. From that infinite space we can call forth all possibilities.

Life coaching as a distinct career

Many roles overlap with the role of life coaching. To some people, a life coach looks like a paid friend. There *is* some overlap between friendship and life coaching, but they are not the same. To other people, a life coach looks like a counselor. Again, there is some overlap, but these two professions are quite distinct.

We could compare life coaches to people in many other roles: managers, supervisors, consultants, rabbis, priests, ministers, sponsors, mentors, teachers, occupational therapists, advice columnists, and even psychics. Knowing distinctions between these roles and life coaching can help you do the job more effectively.

You can get most of these key distinctions by understanding how life coaches differ from both consultants and counselors.

Life coaching is not consulting

Consultants are paid to give advice. For example, a financial consultant advises people about how to handle their money, and a health consultant—a physician—advises people about how to improve their health.

Giving advice has a place, and it is not life coaching. As a life coach, you can talk to people about their finances, their health, their relationships, their career, or any other aspect of their lives—all without giving advice. This attitude toward advice underscores the fundamental difference between consultants and life coaches.

Consultants are paid to share their expertise in a given subject and to recommend certain courses of action. Sometimes, in life, that's valuable and even essential. When I go to a mechanic, I want some clear advice on how to keep my car running. When I go to a physician, I want clear advice on how to keep my body running.

When I go to a life coach, I want something different. I want someone who understands that I can usually generate my own solutions to my own problems. I want someone who realizes that I can create my own goals and discover dozens of ways to achieve them. I want someone who assists me to discover my own passion and unlock my own brilliance. I don't want to leave a life coaching session feeling that my coach is a genius because she gives great advice. I want to leave the session knowing at a deep level that *I* am a genius.

When working with a consultant, I let someone else be the expert on a particular part of my life. When relating to a life coach, *I* get to be the expert on every aspect of my life. That's one way that a life coach empowers me as few consultants can.

Life coaching is not therapy

Life coaches also differ in major ways from social workers, counselors, clinical psychologists, psychiatrists, and other kinds of therapists. Consider the following distinctions:

- Most of a therapist's clients have mental disorders as defined in the *Diagnostic and Statistical Manual of Mental Disorders*. A life coach works mainly with people who have no mental disorders, but when a client does need therapy, they get that in addition to life coaching.
- Therapists often assist people to gain insight by dwelling on the psychodynamics of their thinking and behavior. While life coaches value insight, they assist people to move quickly from the realm of insight into setting goals and taking action.
- Therapy, especially when it's based in psychoanalysis, often delves into the patient's past and inquires into the origins of a behavior. Life coaching is more about assisting clients to change behavior in the present and create the future they want.
- Therapists are often focused on a specific problem—the patient's "presenting issue." Life coaches start with a survey of the client's whole life, including health, relationships, career, spirituality, and much more, and then deal with every aspect of life.

- Therapists often build short-term relationships with patients—perhaps a few weeks or few months. This is especially true in the age of managed care. Life coaches build relationships that last for years, even decades.

- Often a therapist's job can be summarized in the phrase, "There's something wrong that needs fixing." Life coaches are more likely to say, "There's nothing wrong here. My client has a great life and wants it to get even better."

Chapter Two
Mechanics of Life Coaching

Choosing times and ways to meet

Choose times to meet

A coaching session can last anywhere from five minutes to several days. Ask what would forward the client's life right now. With one client, you might meet 10 minutes each day for three weeks to monitor a habit change. With another, you could meet for a whole day to create the first draft of a comprehensive life plan. And with a third client you might meet once each week for two hours. Look to the client as a guide, keeping in mind your own preferred work schedule.

In general, I recommend flexibility in both the timing and length of sessions. I've often spoken to my coach on the phone for five minutes and had a powerful experience. I've also received great value from one-hour, half-day, and full-day sessions.

I also think it's great to call clients between sessions and see how they are doing, or to restate your commitment to hold them in your consciousness and serve them in any way that works. In addition to asking, "How are you?", you might say, "I just want you to know I am thinking about you and wanted to see how you are doing. I also want you to know how much I care about you and how much I am your partner. Remember that if something comes up, we can talk before our next scheduled session."

Choose ways to meet

You can also remain flexible about ways to meet. You can talk over the phone or meet face-to-face. Send letters, faxes, or e-mails.

Sometimes you can even amble through the woods with clients or take a stroll on the beach. One of the most powerful and competent life coaches that I know, Jerry Joiner, regularly takes his clients on walks along the ocean.

People ask me whether there's a qualitative difference between coaching face-to-face and coaching over the phone. My answer is that it depends on the client and the topic. The anonymity of the phone sometimes allows people to reveal more than they do in person. As the coach, when working over the phone, you might feel more comfortable taking detailed notes that can help you pay attention and think clearly. On the other hand, some clients will feel more comfortable with emotional release when they're meeting with you in person. Experiment with all the options and see what works best for each client.

In addition, consider coaching through writing, a medium that coaches tend to under-use. When reading a letter from you, clients can assimilate ideas visually, an option that suits many people's learning styles. Reading also allows clients to absorb messages at their own pace and review them more than once.

Coaching can include more than talking about life. For instance, coaching could mean listening to music with a client. At other times it could mean jogging with clients or running errands with them. Recently, I was on the phone with a client who said that he just felt like meditating, so we were silent together for about three minutes. Another client of mine has sung me several songs over the phone. I think those are all viable options for coaching activities.

Life coaching often takes place in a particular format: a professional life coach who works one-on-one with a bevy of clients over many years, charges each client a monthly retainer, and meets with each client for four to six hours every month. However, this is just one possible format. You can devise any system that works well for you and serves your clients. Following are some variations on this basic coaching format:

- Have more than one life coach. I get coaching from three to five people a month. These people know more about me than anyone else—even more than my mother knew about me. A benefit of having more than one life coach is that I get to experience several different styles of coaching. This kind of diversity keeps the coaching fresh and gives me a lot of ideas that I can bring to my own coaching clients.

- Coach in a triad. For example, Brian coaches Fred, Fred coaches Sharon, and Sharon coaches Brian. In this format, people can trade coaching services. No exchange of money needs to take place. Each person receives coaching, and no one is coaching his or her own coach. This option demonstrates that people can have a coach without incurring any costs.

- Charge for coaching by the hour. I know people who charge as little as $5 per hour to provide this amazing service. Others charge hourly fees ranging from $25 to $100 and more.

- Meet with clients once every one or two months instead of several times each month. Each session can last a half-day, a full day, or several days.

- Offer short-term coaching. For example, someone offered to coach me intensely about a few issues over a period of six months. I chose not to take advantage of the offer, but I think it represents a format that could work for other people.

- Coach mainly over the Internet. Hundreds of people now coach clients mainly through e-mail or computer "chat" sessions where communication takes place via the computer keyboard.

- Coach a group of people. Using this format, you can meet with almost any number of people at one time. Ask one person to step in front of the group and talk about a goal she wants to achieve or a problem she wants to solve. The rest of the people in the room can observe the coaching inter-action and look for ways to apply what they learn to their own lives.

Continue coaching when traveling and on vacation

We don't need to stop our coaching relationship just because the client is traveling or on vacation. Often people need more support in achieving a wonderful life when they are not in their regular routine.

Keep in phone contact with clients throughout the year, no matter where they are. A colleague of mine continued coaching his client as the client took a business trip around the world.

Creating and using a life coaching agreement

Consider creating a life coaching agreement—a document that spells out what you expect of clients and what they can expect from you. This document creates value in several ways. Besides giving you some legal protection, a written agreement can clarify your concept of life coaching and help to define your service.

Following is the life coaching agreement that I have used. **This agreement is a sample only. I do not vouch for its legality**. Please create your own agreement and consider reviewing it with an attorney.

Prior to entering into a life coaching relationship, please carefully read the following agreement and indicate your understanding by signing below:

1. I understand that life coaching is a relationship I have with a life coach (effectiveness coach) that is designed to facilitate the establishment of long-range and short-range goals and the achievement of those goals.

2. I understand that life coaching is designed to be a long-term (multi-year) relationship where the life coach is assisting me to improve the quality of my life.

3. I understand that life coaching is comprehensive in that it deals with almost all areas of my life, including work, finances, education, health, relationships, and entertainment. I acknowledge that deciding on how to handle these issues and implementing my decisions remains my exclusive responsibility.

4. I understand that life coaching is for people who are already basically successful, well-adjusted, and emotionally healthy.

5. I understand that confidentiality in the life coaching relationship is limited. Confidentiality may not apply to certain crimes that have been committed or certain crimes that are being planned. Some crimes may need to be reported to legal authorities. It is also possible that certain topics could be reviewed with other life coaching professionals for training and development purposes.

6. I understand that life coaching does not treat mental disorders as defined specifically in the book titled *Diagnostic and Statistical Manual of Mental Disorders* published by the American Psychiatric Association. If I have anything in my past indicating that I have an unresolved and serious emotional or physical problem, or a mental disorder, then I certify that I am not using life coaching as a substitute for assistance from a mental health professional and/or a medical doctor.

7. I will not use life coaching as a substitute for counseling, psychotherapy, psychoanalysis, mental health care, or substance abuse treatment. I realize that this life coaching is not done by a licensed mental health professional.

8. I promise that if I am currently in therapy or under the care of a mental health professional, that I have consulted with that person regarding the advisability of my working with a life coach.

9. I will not use life coaching in lieu of professional medical advice, legal counsel, accounting assistance, business consultation, or spiritual guidance, and for each of these areas I should consult the appropriate professionals. I acknowledge that I will not use life coaching as a substitute for such professional guidance. I further acknowledge that all decisions on dealing with these issues lies exclusively with me.

Signature   Please print name

Date   Address

City   State   Zip

Getting started with a client

Choosing what to do during the first session with a new client can be challenging. This is a time when you and your clients can exercise full creativity.

Life coaching begins as you build a relationship with your client. This first phase of coaching comes from your heart and your overriding commitment to your client. This is a time to build rapport. This is the time to ask for your client's trust, create an environment for sharing, acknowledge and appreciate your client, and set the stage for creating amazing results.

Summarize the mechanics of coaching

In addition to building relationships, you can do a little "housekeeping" during the first session. Discuss some of the mechanics of life coaching, such as times and ways you intend to meet with your client. Review key policies—your fees, how often you'd like to be paid, how you'd like to be notified about a canceled session, and so on. This is an excellent time to review your life coaching agreement. Talking about logistics helps people get comfortable and lays the foundation for future sessions.

Ask what your client wants from the first session

Start with the obvious: Ask clients what they want from their first meeting with you.

Usually, I go into an initial session knowing what *I* want to get out of it—for example, a list of the client's key values, a survey of his effectiveness in several areas of life, the names of his family members, and the like. Those are some of my goals. In addition, I want to take the time to learn the client's goal for that first session.

From the beginning, you can enlist your clients' thoughts and allow him to cocreate the coaching relationship with you.

Survey your client's life

One great way to start a life coaching relationship is to guide clients through a survey of what's working well—and not working well—in each area of their lives. Ask people to be completely honest with you about the current state of their relationships, their health, their finances, their spirituality, and more.

This activity brings to mind Step Four of Alcoholics Anonymous, which asks for a "searching and fearless moral inventory." The key idea is for your client to be comprehensive and to tell the truth.

Clients can do this survey in many ways, both formal and informal. One option is for them to fill out the survey in *Human Being: A Manual For Happiness, Health, Love, and Wealth,* the book I wrote with Stan Lankowitz. This survey guides readers to consider their lives as a whole, celebrating what they love about their lives and reflecting on what behaviors and circumstances they'd like to change. In addition, feel free to create and use your own written survey.

You can also conduct verbal surveys with clients. While taking notes, request information with brief questions and statements such as, "To begin, just tell me a little about how your relationships are going…. Okay, now describe your current state of health…. Now let's talk about your relationship with money…. Next, how do you feel about your use of alcohol and other drugs?…. Okay, now tell me about how your work's going…. In general, what's missing in your life? And, what do you particularly enjoy about your life?"

Doing a survey often leads logically to another wonderful activity for a first session: goal setting. One option is to make a long list of what clients have just been putting up with in life—for example, a dead-end job, a lingering resentment, a troubled relationship, or a perpetually unfinished project.

Ask clients to generate goals in each area of their personal and professional lives. With your assistance, they can start with short-term possibilities and then stretch out further in time, creating goals for five, ten, and even twenty years into the future. This process is described in detail in *Creating Your Future: Five Steps to the Life of Your Dreams.*

Another option, provided you have the necessary training and materials, is to give new clients a formal assessment. Examples include the Myers-Briggs® Personality Profile and the Strong® Vocational Interest Inventory. These inventories can categorize people in ways that could be limiting. They are only two of many ways to learn information about a client.

Surveys and assessments create value in several ways. Besides revealing key information about clients, these tools can help clients get past the illusion that they have little to work on ("Everything about my life is going just fine"). When surveys lead to a long list of goals to be accomplished over months or years, they also reinforce the value of a long-term relationship with a life coach.

Of course, you don't have to do a survey during the first session. Like everything else I say about coaching, take this idea as a guideline, not as a rule. Some clients may come in with a specific and timely agenda for life coaching.

Ask about conflicts between values and behaviors

One method for getting to know clients is asking them what they most value. If that seems too abstract, try phrasing the question this way: "What is most important to you—and most difficult for you—to keep foremost?" For example, clients might say that they value exercise but seldom make time for this activity. They might value taking regular vacations, spending time with their children, reading, and countless other activities that they forget about or do only rarely.

Here is an opportunity for you to reaffirm your commitment to each client. When clients confess how they have trouble keeping first things first, offer your continual service: "You can count on me to be a person who keeps your values foremost in mind and assists you to live them in your daily life."

Ask for complaints and celebrations

Right off the bat, you can ask clients to complain. Getting in touch with their complaints can quickly reveal what people really want. If people complain about their lack of energy, that probably means they want more energy. If they complain about having too many debts, then they probably want to get out of debt. And if they complain about feeling lonely, that's a clue they want to meet more people or have more intimate relationships with people they already know. With your coaching, clients can turn each complaint into a specific goal with action plans—plans for increasing their energy level, reducing debt, making friends, and much more.

Also ask for celebrations. Your client might say, "I just appreciate how well I'm getting along with my wife right now." In response, you can take a few minutes to celebrate how well this part of the client's life is working. Then suggest to him that he might invent a plan for maintaining this wonderful relationship.

Listen a lot and go longer

I recommend that in every coaching session—particularly the first one—you listen, listen, and then listen some more. Often you don't need to prepare a full agenda for this initial meeting since many clients will come pretty well prepared with an agenda of their own.

Allow some extra time for that first session to get the most out of it. You can set aside a half-day, full day, or even two days to get started with a new client. This strategy offers at least two benefits: you get to learn a lot about the client and clients get a sense that they've embarked on something that's big and life transforming.

Preparing for sessions

Part of your effectiveness as a life coach hinges on your process for preparing to meet with each client. Over time, you'll discover what works for you and for your clients.

Renew your commitment

One way to begin your preparation is to ground yourself in your fundamental commitment to your client's success and fulfillment. You can do this in any way that's meaningful for you.

Often, I visualize the person I am going to talk to and remember my commitment to that person. Then I look to see if there is something I could do before the call that would make the call more powerful.

Review your notes

Before you meet with a client, review the notes you've taken from previous sessions.

I recommend that you take a lot of notes during each session and let clients know that you are doing so. Effective notes help you to remember the details of clients' lives, hold each client in your consciousness between sessions, and to remind clients of what they've said. Assure clients that any notes you take are confidential.

Set an agenda and be willing to scrap it

There's power in creating a large agenda for a coaching session, one that's much too big to accomplish in a single call or meeting. Having an exciting agenda that's only half-completed creates a demand for the next session.

Agenda items can include anything you do in the context of your life coaching relationship—surveys, goal setting, problem-solving, rituals, celebrations, and much more.

Remind clients that they don't have to wait for the next session to tackle unfinished agenda items. At any point between sessions they can record insights, write goals, and carry out their plans. Invite clients to take their favorite idea or intention from each session and run with it.

Agendas work well when you hold them lightly. At times, you may follow your written agenda to a "T." At other times, you can serve clients most by scrapping the agenda and following the client's lead in the moment. Often, what unfolds is something that's bigger and more important than what you'd planned.

In addition, some clients will come with a bottom-line agenda of their own: "Okay, here's what I want today. Please assist me with this right now." When that happens, you don't have to warm up to the coaching by asking the client for a general check-in first ("Well, before we get started, how are you?"). Some people come in to session with a clear idea of what they want, and they just want to get rolling.

This is a wonderful aspect of coaching—the varying pace of it. Clients come in with their own cadence, be it slow or fast or some-thing in-between. This variation in the way that clients move into the agenda creates spontaneity and aliveness in the life coaching relationship.

Get into the "zone"

Another way to prepare for coaching sessions is to remember times when you were particularly effective with clients. Recall in detail the times you coached people well. Bring to mind the specific people and circumstances that were involved. Recreating these experiences in your mind can instantly put you in the "zone" for coaching—feeling pumped with energy and ready to create.

your client to prepare

Some of the best preparation for a coaching session can occur when your client takes the time to look at what she wants during that time. I ask all of my clients to take up to an hour prior to our time together and fill out the following form. I also ask them to email this to me at least two hours before our session. This gives the client a chance to reflect on what she wants and gives me a chance to get up to date about that client before our meeting.

This form (and most of my coaching sessions) begins with celebration.

Once the coaching session is complete, I ask the client to spend five to ten minutes reflecting on our time together and send me their discoveries and intentions.

I recommend that you modify this form to fit your particular coaching style.

COACHING PREPARATION FORM

- What wins, celebrations, or accomplishments have occurred since our last conversation?

_____

_____

_____

- What did not get done that you intended to do?

_____

_____

_____

- What challenges are you currently facing (or complaints do you have, or what energy-drainers are currently in your life)?

_____

_____

_____

- What do you want from our coaching today?

_____

_____

_____

- Once the session is completed, write down what you have learned and what you intend to do as a result of our time together. Complete each of the following statements one or more times:

I learned (or relearned) that I …

I intend (or promise) to …

Staying focused during sessions

As a life coach, you tell clients that you want to assist them in all areas of life. Then one of your clients says, "You know, I'm just not traveling enough." Then you start thinking, *Well, I'm not traveling enough either.* Another client says, "I'm just not having the kind of relationship I want with my spouse." And you think to yourself, *Wow, neither am I.*

These are some examples of how we can get "hooked." My concern is that once we're hooked, we stop being present to the client. All of a sudden we're working on our own lives instead of focusing on the client.

There are two separate questions here. First, how do I know when I'm hooked and no longer grounded in serving the client? Second, once I know I'm hooked, what do I do about it? Those are both great questions for life coaches to consider.

Commit to be present

Before applying any specific techniques to stay focused during coaching sessions, just commit to be fully present with each client. With this commitment, you can make moment-to-moment choices to align with this commitment and release distractions as they occur.

Pay attention to your attention

You can set up an early warning system for distraction by checking in on your attention frequently. Be attentive to your attention, aware of your awareness, conscious of your consciousness. When you are, you will notice that you drift off.

We all do this at times. And when we are drifting, then we are probably not effective coaches.

You might find that your attention consistently drifts to certain concerns: *How am I doing? How do I look? Does this client like me? Does he think I am creating value?* All that is distraction from focusing on the client's well being.

I find that it's almost always enough to just notice my distraction. Then I can gently bring myself back to the client. And there's no need to judge myself for being distracted. Just recognizing that I've drifted and gently refocusing my attention is sufficient.

You might find your attention drifting during longer sessions with clients when you are doing a lot of focused listening and feel tired. This is a great opportunity to practice bringing your attention back to the client, moment-by-moment. When your thinking wanders away from the client—into the past, the future, or to your own assessment of your current state—then you're likely to feel even more tired. The more you are fully present to what's going on with your client, the less room there is in your mind for thoughts such as *I'm exhausted*.

Ask clients to repeat themselves

When you get distracted and miss something that a client says, you can ask clients to repeat themselves: "I'm not sure I heard that fully. Would you say it again?" Repetition is not only good for you, clients often gain valuable insights just by repeating themselves.

Write a distraction card

Another option for focusing attention is to write yourself a note. Start by grabbing a 3x5 card. On one side of the card, jot yourself a note describing your distraction—*My own relationship with my spouse; Not enough travel; Need milk*, or whatever it is. You might find that once you write the briefest note, you're suddenly focused again. The distraction has vanished.

Often, I take the card, put it in my pocket, and file it away for later. That way I can tell my consciousness not to worry: *You don't have to keep reminding me about this topic every five minutes. When I go home and empty my pockets tonight, I'll find that card.*

Write an action plan

If I'm distracted, I occasionally ask to put my client on hold for a moment while I write a card. Then I flip the card over, and on the other side I write down an action plan for handling the distraction. That plan could be as simple as *Call Sara later today* or *Stop by the dry cleaner's on the way home from work*. In a few seconds, the distraction is handled, and I'm focused on the client again.

Report distraction

You might even choose to report distractions to your clients. Just confess. When you try all of the techniques listed above and your attention still drifts, you can just be forthright and tell on yourself: "You know, I'm drifting, so let me take a second to refocus on you."

You don't need to go into a long explanation about why you're distracted ("When you started talking about your spouse, I started thinking about mine, and that's all I'm focused on right now, and I'm finding it so hard to be with you because I'm in this conflict with her and....") Instead, you can just give the basic message: "I want to tell you that I've not been paying close attention to you for the last several moments. And, my commitment is to be here, so tell me again what you just said and let's keep going."

Schedule another time

At times, you might apply all the strategies I've mentioned and find that none of them really do the trick. If that happens, consider reporting the depth of your distraction and asking the client to schedule another meeting time.

Hold this option as a last resort. Clients have set up this time to be with you, and they expect something powerful from you. But renegotiating the time is far more effective than being with a client only in pretense.

Taking notes

Whenever you listen to a client, I recommend that you take notes. Remind clients that you keep notes confidential and take them only to assist memory.

Take notes consciously

One of the qualities of a master coach is the ability to keep conscious notes—clear, high quality notes. Include whatever content you'd like to refer to in the future. And even if you never come back to these notes, the mere act of writing them down drives them deeper into your consciousness.

You can create a note-taking format that works for you. For example, write down specific points to make or questions to ask a client. In my notes, I usually draw a line in front of the ideas that I want to speak to the client about and then check off each item after covering it during a session. One benefit of this format is that I can review the things I intended to say during a session but didn't get to and carry them forward to the next session.

Present your notes to the client

Your notes can create direct value for the people you coach. While clients define a problem, brainstorm options, or speak a series of goals, you can take detailed notes and then present them to clients.

This strategy has really helped me as a coaching client. When I was looking at whether to sell a company that I had started and run for 12 years, I spent a lot of time with a coach exploring the pros and cons. My coach didn't say much, but he did take a lot of notes and gave them to me. I reviewed those notes, extracted my arguments for each option, and typed them up in an organized way. If I'd tried to take such detailed notes while my ideas were flowing freely, I would have been doing two things at once—and probably doing neither of them effectively.

This technique can also work wonders when clients are dealing with emotionally charged communication. One of my clients was having serious problems with her husband. In response, I asked her to first imagine that her husband was in the room with us. Then I asked her to tell her husband everything that she'd been withholding from him—everything that from her point of view had not been working about their relationship. While she spoke, I took notes.

As we continued, my client became brilliant—about three pages worth of brilliant! I wrote down each of her points, then reviewed each one using her own words whenever possible. In turn, that triggered her to say even more, and I wrote that down also. She left the session with the essence of her communication in writing, which was even more powerful than just having the opportunity to speak. She then reviewed my notes, organized them, and communicated the key points to her husband in less than 15 minutes. This was a benefit to him; he didn't have to listen to sometimes garbled or even inaccurate communication. Instead, he got the kernels of his wife's truth.

Write and feed back your client's exact words

I believe that, in large part, our words create our lives. More specifically, our words create our actions, and our actions create our circumstances.

Given the importance of our words, it's amazing that we live in a culture that doesn't value words much. People spend their language as if words are cheap. They say, "I'll meet you at 5" and then don't. They say, "I'll send that to you" and then don't. What's more, they say, "I'm no good at my job" when they know they are, or, "I just don't care" when they clearly do.

We can assist clients to value their words. And one way we can do that is to write down those words. Then we can hand our notes over to clients, or retype those notes and send them to clients. We can even give clients several copies of their words so they can post those copies in places such as a desk, a bathroom mirror, or a refrigerator door. In each case, when we write another person's words, we give those words more visibility and importance.

I've developed a habit of writing down the words that people around me speak, giving those words back to them, and sometimes even framing key quotations. For example, on March 3, 1997, my coworker and friend Bill Rentz said: "I see that all there is for me to do is celebrate life, and all the work I do can be a means to that end. My purpose each day is to figure out how I can celebrate life even more." Years ago, my assistant, Robbie Murchison, said: "We can be leery about giving ourselves to anything that takes less than a lifetime to accomplish."

A couple of guidelines can help you get the most from this strategy. First, write clients' words periodically, not all the time. Also, encourage clients to take their own notes. Anything that you write down can supplement—not replace—what they write.

Sometimes when I talk, especially in an emotionally charged situation, I'm not sure that I'm always making sense. I might feel a little crazy. But if someone takes what I say and gives it back to me in writing, then I often know what I've learned, what I want, and what I intend to do next.

Completing sessions

Suggest assignments

One way you can assist clients to carry their insights and intentions beyond the coaching session and into their daily lives is to suggest assignments.

41

Assignments can be as varied as your creativity allows. For example: *Consider writing at least 20 new outcomes you want in terms of your health.... Please log the number of times that you feel antagonistic during the next week.... How about if you choose one day this week to ignore your to-do list and do whatever you're moved to do in the moment.... Get a bid from three contractors for that work.... Eat one meal each day alone in meditative silence.* These are just a few possibilities.

To enhance the value of assignments:

- Give assignments in the spirit of possibility and suggestion. If a client doesn't like the first option you present, then offer several alternatives.
- Follow up at the next session. When clients don't do assignments, avoid judging them ("How can I coach you if you fail to do assignments?"). Instead of making people wrong, trust the possible genius in their choice. Also, consider doing the assignment with the client during the coaching session, or, carry over the assignment to the next session. You can even use uncompleted assignments as fuel for insights: "What did you notice about yourself in relation to this assignment? Perhaps that you don't have time or that you procrastinate. If you like, we can discuss that today."
- Ask clients to create an agenda for the next coaching session. This is a wonderful standing assignment.
- Encourage clients to generate their own assignments.

Write a letter

I have written many letters to coaching clients, reviewing our last contact and previewing the next session.

In addition to regular mail, you can use faxes or e-mails for this kind of communication. The speed of these media can make it easy to stay in frequent contact with clients between sessions.

Ask for reflection and commitment

At the end of most of my coaching sessions, I ask the client to take a few minutes and complete the last section of the Coaching Preparation Form mentioned earlier in this chapter. Then the client completes one or more discovery and intention statements.

Discovery statements take the form of "I discovered that …," or "I rediscovered that I …," or "I learned that I …," or "I relearned that I …". These statements assist the client to reflect on the coaching session and gain insight into his life.

Given that coaching is more about action than insight, intention statements are designed to get the client in touch with his commitments. They take the form "I intend to…," or "I promise to …".

Ending the life coaching relationship

There could come a time when a client says, "I'm just not getting value from what we're doing." Or you may recognize that there's no value being created in your coaching sessions. In response, you can offer to change the content of the coaching, or to change the coaching process, or both—or you could just stop coaching the client.

Keep in mind that coaching relationships do not have to end only when the coaching seems ineffective. I coached one of my clients for almost two years before we stopped. This client acknowledged my skills and me more than I have ever been acknowledged by anyone. He also said that from his point of view our coaching simply was complete for now, and that was fine with me.

When ending a coaching relationship, keep in mind the following suggestions.

Remember that you don't need any one client

As you gain confidence in your marketing skills, you can feel more comfortable about ending your coaching with a client. If you are confident that you can find new clients at any time, then you don't need to continue coaching any client for financial reasons. You might want 10 clients in order to make a living, but you don't have to *need* any one of them. That way, if a client chooses to quit, you don't have to take it personally or view the event as a crisis.

Refer the client

With one of my clients, I just couldn't get to the point where I saw him as a loving, generous, and creative human being. I got my own coaching on this issue from two people, yet my vision of this person stayed basically the same. Since my definition of coaching includes holding clients in high regard, I chose to stop going through the motions of coaching him, and instead, I referred him to another coach.

Whenever your best professional judgment is that you're not making a difference with a client, consider ending the coaching relationship. In some cases, you can serve clients more by referring them to a mental health professional, physician, or some other consultant. After reflecting on your effectiveness with these clients and taking whatever insights you can from coaching them, you can simply assist these people to get on with the next chapter of their personal growth and development.

Ask for appreciations and reflections

When you end coaching relationships, consider asking these clients to take a retroactive look at their coaching experience. Give them one final assignment: to write down all they've learned and appreciated about your coaching relationship. Besides giving you powerful feedback, this writing can highlight how much clients have changed while working with you.

I did this review when I completed with one of my coaches, and it was great. After I communicated to him how much I learned through our relationship, we both cried. I took this as both a celebration and an acknowledgment.

Accepting acknowledgment from your client is a powerful way to end the life coaching. If clients leave without fully acknowledging you and knowing that you've received that acknowledgment, then they could feel incomplete. They could go for months or years sensing that they still owe you an expression of appreciation. It's sufficient for most people if they know that they thanked you well and that you received that thanks.

Create a ceremony

When completing a coaching relationship, you and your client can create value by inventing some kind of ceremony to mark the occasion. You could go out for dinner, have a picnic in the park, go to a concert, or go for a walk in the woods. You could schedule a meeting where you write each other a letter while you're sitting together. You could also give each other a poster or trophy, or climb to the top of a hill or mountain to bury some symbol of your relationship, meditate together, or perform some other symbolic ritual.

These kinds of rituals and celebrations, even when they're informal, are important for giving people a sense of closure. And when you complete a relationship that's as close as the one between client and life coach, I think that closure assists everyone involved.

Begin another kind of relationship

You can turn the end of a coaching relationship into the beginning of another kind of relationship. Even though you may stop coaching a person, you could still be in contact in other roles, whether that be as friends, business associates, colleagues, or something else.

If you choose this option, talk about how you want to reposition the relationship. For years, I had a close relationship with a therapist. When we ended that form of relationship, I didn't know how to relate to her: Do I still write to her? Do I just send her Christmas cards? Do I never contact her again? I just didn't know what she expected or even what I wanted for our new relationship.

You can prevent that kind of ambiguity with former clients by defining your new roles and choosing the ways you want to interact.

Assist the client to move into the future

When completing a coaching a relationship, you could say, "I know we are finishing, and I think that works great. Now, tell me about your future. What will you do to ensure that you live the life you've dreamed of living? What structures are you going to set up to keep your plan alive? Do you have another person you can bring into your life like a coach?" In this way of completing a coaching relationship, you keep the future alive.

Chapter Three
The Coaching Continuum

The continuum—an overview

Among managers, counselors, and coaches there are distinct schools of thought about how to empower people. Some managers are directive. Others are "hands-off" and they just point out the overall direction and let employees figure out the rest. Likewise, some counselors routinely direct their conversations with clients. Then there are counselors such as Carl Rogers who believe that people can solve their own problems when they are listened to completely and affirmed.

This range of opinion also exists in the coaching profession. I like to describe this range as the *coaching continuum*. You can use this continuum as a way to define coaching and as a tool for enrolling life coaching clients.

The coaching continuum ranges from the least directive responses at the top (listen fully and affirm) to the most directive technique at the bottom (offer an option):

- Listen fully and affirm
- Listen fully and feed back celebrations, dreams, and action plans
- Ask the client to generate a few new possibilities
- Ask the client to generate many possibilities
- Add to the client's list of possibilities
- Present at least 10 possibilities (some contradictory)
- Present at least 3 possibilities
- Teach a new technique
- Offer an option

- Give advice
- Give advice by sharing or questioning
- Give the answer

The dotted line indicates the boundary between coaching and giving advice. Though there is a time and place for advice, I want to draw a clear distinction between advising and coaching. In a life coaching relationship, advice has little value and can even be counter-productive.

More details about each of these levels on the coaching continuum follow.

The continuum in detail

Listen fully and affirm

At the top of the coaching continuum is a unique way of being with people that I call "full listening." Sometimes what really makes sense is to just affirm clients and listen to them empathetically—period. We can trust that clients will create the life that they want when we simply listen and remain totally committed to their success. Full listening is an invitation for people to discover their passion—a ticket into the client's soul and a magnet that draws out brilliance. New coaches commonly feel like they should earn their money by doing more than listening. They want to be helpful; they want to contribute. Sometimes during a life coaching session they have something valuable to say and they can't wait to say it. When that happens, what's probably waiting is a piece of advice. I claim that we can often contribute more by sitting on our hands, biting our tongues, and just listening fully.

When working with one of my own life coaches over the past several years, I spoke about 98 percent of the time. But, the 2 percent of the time that my coach did speak was both effective and extraordinary.

Once we are fully committed to the success of our clients, our next job as life coaches is full and complete listening. You can learn to create this soulful listening—the kind of listening where you're moved to the depth of your being by what another person says.

When they reveal their most intimate thoughts and feelings, what most people want us to do is just receive what they're revealing. They don't want our advice. They don't want our help. They don't want us to fix them. They just want us to "get it." At these times, our opportunity is to practice the rare skill of full listening.

Full listening and affirming begins as a technique and can grow into an all-pervasive way of being. The following suggestions can assist you to grow in this way.

BE QUIET

You can begin by just listening. Don't speak beyond an "uh huh" or a nod. Be quiet mentally as well as verbally. Avoid listening with your answer running—thinking about how you want to respond to what the client says. Release each moment-to-moment distraction and simply return to the client. Notice any pull to stop listening and any desire to start talking, then remember that coaching is often about letting people talk and then they will get clear.

When you listen fully, there's not much to do. Just listen, listen, and then listen some more. Keep listening until the client seems to be completely done speaking. At that point, you can speak just long enough to ask, "Is there anything else you want to say about that?" Clients will tell you when they're done.

OPEN YOUR BODY TO RECEIVING

Full listening involves a total body response. You become soft, both physically and mentally, and free of resistance.

If you have a strong emotional response to the client's message and find it difficult to listen fully, see if you can resume that bodily posture of full listening. Notice how you're sitting and how you're breathing. Open up your eyes and look into the client's eyes with an attention that is both focused and relaxed.

SPEAK WHEN YOU NOTICE YOU'RE NOT LISTENING

When we pretend to listen, people notice. Clients know when our attention is focused, just as they can tell when a massage therapist is fully attending to their muscles.

Don't pretend to listen. If you start to lose focus—if you're confused, bored, sleepy, or distracted—then say so. You can even pinpoint where and when you got lost: "I followed you up to the point where you started talking about money, and then I got lost." Making this kind of confession can contribute to clients. If you're lost, then it's possible that their thinking is not as clear as it could be. By speaking again so that you can understand, clients can gain clarity.

Telling the truth can unleash reserves of energy that you can channel back into listening. Even if you still don't feel like listening, you model self-disclosure and authentic speaking to your clients.

NOTICE AND RELEASE JUDGMENTS

Nearly every moment we're awake, there's a voice inside our heads that offers a constant commentary. For much of the time, that voice offers judgments on people and events: "This is boring." "He's silly." "I've heard this a hundred times before." When we let that voice take charge of our awareness, our ability to listen fully is compromised.

Trying to fight this judgmental voice gives it power. A more viable option is to just notice the voice without taking it seriously. Then you can gently release what the voice says.

Though you don't have to take the judgmental voice seriously, I do recommend that you take your actions seriously. Even when that mental voice gets louder, you can keep your lips closed and refrain from voicing judgments. Your behavior can show that you're listening non-judgmentally even while the judgmental voice is trying to get your attention.

Eventually, the judgmental voice will start to quiet, particularly if you just acknowledge that it's there and don't try to resist it. As you apply this suggestion to release judgments, you may notice that the judgmental voice begins to soften and turns into one that says, "This person sounds like a jerk right now, but I know pretty soon he's going to be brilliant again."

I also find it helps to practice with circumstances that trigger my judgments. One of the techniques that I've experimented with for twenty years is to go out in nature, seek out things that I find hard to experience and then practice acceptance. For example, I might study a dead animal filled with maggots lying on the side of a road. I stay in the presence of that sight until I can move toward loving it—that is, permit it and allow it.

I also apply this practice to people whom I find difficult to love. Rather than avoiding them or speaking my judgments, I want to approach them with a deep, soulful acceptance and then just keep listening, being with them, and moving toward my commitment to love them.

ACCEPT NON-ACCEPTANCE

Suppose that you've committed to listening fully and affirming. Then a client walks into a session and makes a blatantly racist comment such as: "I hate black people. They're just a bunch of lazy, good-for-nothing criminals. They threaten our whole way of life. And the only way to stop them is to avoid contact with them or just get rid of them."

If you're like most coaches I know, you'll immediately face the dilemma of how to reconcile this statement with your commitment to allow, embrace, and affirm each client.

Many people would draw the line at this point and say, "I could never work with such a bigoted human being, let alone love that person or listen fully to him and affirm his view of the world."

In response, I say that we can look for ways to practice full listening with whomever shows up in our lives—even the blatantly racist client or others whom we find equally difficult to accept. I believe that when people fully express and explore their racist attitudes, they can eventually move beyond those attitudes. Racism and other forms of non-acceptance can be a place that people pass through on their way to a higher plane. If we coach from the assumption that racism is not inbred or permanent, then we can make a difference even with these clients. We can learn to accept non-acceptance in a way that transforms people.

Keep in mind that if you are unable to hold the client in high regard, you always have the option to end the coaching relationship. Also, remember that you can listen fully to people and accept them even when you don't agree with what they say or do. You could say something like the following:

"So, what you see here is a group of people who threaten your whole way of life—the culture you want to preserve and the future that you want for your family. I got it. Given how you view the world, I can see where you'd choose to avoid all contact with these people. And, I can see that this choice absolutely makes sense to you. I think that many people would make the same choice if they viewed the world in the same way.

"Now, I want to tell you that I feel some upset about what you're saying. I've never coached someone who's felt this way about African-American people and it is not how I feel, so this is difficult for me.

"I also want to know more about the culture that you want to preserve and the future you want for your family. My job as a life coach is to help you unlock your passion, so tell me more about this vision of yours."

Please understand that I will do everything I can to prevent discrimination against African-American people or any other group. In the same way, I will do everything I can to stop rape, even if that means putting myself in physical danger. And, I can take these actions even as I listen fully and affirm the rapist and the racist in the way I've just described.

CLEAR YOUR MIND AND RENEW YOUR ENERGY

When you listen fully, you can easily get "filled up" with everything clients say about their hopes, dreams, passions, and goals. You might feel burned out with little mental space or physical energy for full listening. At these times, even your sincere commitment to clients may not be enough to sustain your full listening.

Before this happens, you can find ways to create mental space, renew your energy, and move back to a place where you can listen fully and affirm. Experiment with the following suggestions:

- *Debrief.* If you want to create a space to listen, then talk. When you don't feel like listening, you might find that you desperately want to be heard. Find someone who will listen as you speak about what you've been thinking, feeling, and doing in the last few days or weeks. That person can be a family member, friend, coach, or even your client. You can also debrief by writing in your journal or leaving a voice mail message for someone who cares about you.

- *Do something to clear your mind.* Meditate, exercise, listen to music, or take a walk in nature.

- *Make time for fun.* Before a coaching session, treat yourself to a delicious meal, a hot bath, or something else that you find deeply enjoyable.

- *Recall miracles.* Remember the times that coaching led to breakthroughs in clients' lives.

- *Be willing to hold each client in your consciousness as a brilliant, lovable, and creative human being.* Adopting this viewpoint can renew your energy for listening fully.

- *Step into your client's shoes for a minute.* Remember how tremendous it feels to receive the gift of deep, soulful listening.

- *Breathe.* Do a "hit" of oxygen. Take slow, deep breaths to calm your mind and relieve stress. Or, energize yourself with a series of quick inhalations and exhalations. Oxygen is a great natural drug, and you can literally get high on it.

- *Clarify your intention.* Prior to a coaching session, take time to write down your agenda for this session as well as your larger vision and long-term goals for working with the client.

COMMIT TO FULL LISTENING BEFORE YOU KNOW HOW

We could apply all of the techniques described above and still not listen fully. What I've listed so far are just strategies, but they don't really explain how to listen. I don't know if any of us really know how we do anything. My best guess is that the way we do anything flows from commitment.

If you want to listen fully, then commit from the depth of your soul that you're here to love and accept people, and then practice that commitment.

When people ask me how to change a habit, I suggest that they commit to the change, monitor their behavior, and practice, practice, practice without reproach. The same process applies to full listening—just commit to be loving, accepting, allowing, and permitting, and then practice.

Of course, I've made lots of mistakes while practicing full listening, and periodically I still make mistakes. When that happens, I just return to my commitment.

When someone listens fully to me it seems like one of the most empowering gifts that another person can give me, so I want to give that gift back to people. The life coaching strategy that I use more than any other is to simply commit to full listening and then practice.

Listen fully and feed back celebrations, dreams, and actions

One of my clients separated from her husband and felt stuck with a large number of major decisions to make. When meeting with her, I said little and affirmed much. I just listened about 95 percent of the time and simply fed back what she said. This woman reported that our time together was very powerful.

This is an example of the next level down on the coaching continuum. At this level, you practice full and complete listening and occasionally report to clients some of what you hear them say. Specifically, you feed back the client's celebrations (even when they are few and far between). Also, listen for what the client wants—their dreams—and mirror them back to the client. You can also listen for action plans.

The idea is to summarize the essence of what you hear and ch
out your summary for accuracy. This is like active listening—ho...
ing up a mirror to clients so that they can see themselves with
greater clarity. The difference between this type of active listening
and a textbook definition of active listening is that you are not
feeding back everything. Rather, you are a mirror that is only
reflecting what the client likes (celebrations), what the client wants
(dreams), and the ways the client imagines fulfilling his dreams
(actions).

At this level of the continuum, you can occasionally ask questions
to verify that you're receiving the client's message accurately.
Asking these questions can help clients clarify their thinking.

Questions can also backfire. Whenever you ask a question, however
subtly, you are managing the conversation. With practice, you can
tell the difference between questions that clarify and questions that
take clients in a direction they haven't chosen. Powerful coaching is
usually directed by the client. So, ask questions consciously and
with care.

Ask the client to generate a few new possibilities

As you descend one more level down the continuum, you become a
little more directive. In addition to feeding back some of what you
hear and asking a few questions, you ask your client to generate a
few new possibilities. These possibilities could include options
additional celebrations, dreams, or action plans.

At this point on the continuum, you might say:

- Tell me two or three more ways you could solve that.
- What are a few things you could do to overcome obstacles to
  reaching this goal?
- What else is working in your life?
- What else do you want?
- If you were really happy about this, how would it look?
- Are there other resources you can draw on to solve this problem?

When some people hear about this level of the coaching continuum, they object that clients don't need a life coach to invent new possibilities; clients can generate possibilities on their own.

The problem is, clients don't. Many of us are not acculturated to generate lots of solutions to any given problem. We're not trained to sit down, think, and sustain that kind of inquiry. Assisting clients to stay in this inquiry is a key value that life coaches create.

Your skills at full listening can still apply at this level. When a client is thinking of options, avoid adding to the client's list of possibilities or evaluating any of them. Just listen.

Ask your client to generate many possibilities

The more possibilities you request clients to invent, the more directive you become. At times this request can serve clients—and, it is one more step away from just listening fully. For this reason, I see asking for many possibilities as another step along the continuum.

While presenting to many kinds of audiences, I have done an exercise that illustrates this level. I ask people to pick the toughest, most persistent problem in their lives and describe it in writing. Then I ask them to list 20 solutions to that problem—including 5 especially powerful solutions that can be implemented immediately. At the end of my presentation, most people report that their problem is handled. My role is just to keep asking for invention: "What could you do to solve this? Great! Now, what's something else that you could do?"

While coaching, you can ask clients to voice a possibility even if it seems crazy. Suppose a client says, "One way I could resolve the conflict with my mother-in-law is to kill her." You can take a possibility this wild and look for a way to make it "right." For example, you could suggest that one way of "killing" his mother-in-law would be to release all his *images* of his mother-in-law based on past interactions with her.

As a coach, your job is to affirm all the solutions that a client generates. With occasional modification, there is a gem of wisdom in almost every idea.

Add to your client's list of possibilities

At the next level along the coaching continuum, you add to the client's list of possibilities. This means that you become slightly more directive. In addition to listening fully, feeding back, and asking the client to generate options, you generate some possibilities of your own.

When you add to your client's list of possibilities, you reach a key level on the continuum. At this level, some of the focus moves away from your client's creativity and shifts to *your* creativity. Though this shift can contribute to clients, it does mean that clients are being less self-generative.

Present at least 10 possibilities (some contradictory)

To get even more directive, you can generate a long list of possibilities for your client: "Although I won't give you advice, here are 10 possibilities for you to consider." Clients can then review your list and choose which possibilities they might want to implement.

At this level, you are still giving clients an opportunity to be self-generative: In your list, include possibilities that contradict each other. The value of contradiction is that clients must think for themselves to select among options.

You can even give bizarre possibilities along with the reasonable ones: "Some ways for you to lose weight include walking across the country or wiring your jaw shut." Then ask your client, "If these possibilities don't work, then what are some that *could* work?"

POSSIBILITIES WITH A SENSE OF POSSIBILITY

There's a danger that when you present possibilities, clients will hear them as directive suggestions. To prevent this, let your speaking and way of being reinforce a sense of possibility. Then clients can receive your ideas as options, not directives. When that happens, you are coaching on the continuum toward the level of possibility and away from the level of advice.

Clients can use your possibilities as a springboard for their own creativity. By bumping up against our ideas, clients can create their own. When you suggest that a client could work only part-time within two weeks, she might say no. But then she might see that she could switch to part-time work within two months or even two years.

PRESENT POSSIBILITIES AS STATEMENTS, NOT QUESTIONS

People will find it easier to decline an option when you present it as a statement rather than a question. A statement can be left hanging, but a question calls for a response. For example, the statement "You could eliminate chocolate from your diet" does not require a response. But the question "Would you like to eliminate chocolate from your diet?" almost forces the client to take a stand.

In our society, most people think it's only polite to answer questions. Declining to answer a question calls for an unusual degree of assertiveness.

PRESENT POSSIBILITIES WITHOUT ATTACHMENT

It's key that you present possibilities lightly—without attachment. You're presenting possibilities as long as you are not upset whenever the client says "no" to one of your ideas.

If we're attached to an idea, clients know. And in response they can become guarded, feel resigned, stop thinking for themselves, start being defensive, or—worse yet—follow our "advice."

PRESENT PRACTICAL POSSIBILITIES

For years, it's been my intent whenever I write, teach, or coach people to present specific strategies and techniques—methods and procedures that people can actually put into practice, often immediately. I have a long-standing commitment to avoid being theoretical and to avoid rambling.

Speaking in an organized way and presenting a series of clear points aids clients in making choices and taking action.

AVOID FAVORING CERTAIN POSSIBILITIES

I am leery of recommending one possibility to clients as better than another. If I do this, I am then giving advice and acting as a consultant. I don't want to enroll clients in a particular way of thinking or sell them on a certain alternative. Instead, I want to invite them to consider a number of possibilities. If the invitation is clear, concise, and authentic, then clients will know which ideas make sense for them.

Present at least three possibilities

Instead of presenting 10 or more possibilities to clients, you can put fewer ideas out on the table.

Whenever I present fewer possibilities, I do so with the knowledge that I'm being more directive. That means that I've just moved one more level on the coaching continuum.

The problem with giving just two or three possibilities is that many people will think you just gave them the answer to a question, the solution to their problem. They might say to themselves, "Now we're getting close! My coach just gave me three ideas instead of ten. If I can just figure out which two he's not really recommending, then my problem is solved."

You can minimize the chance of this outcome by presenting at least one possibility that contradicts one or more of the others. You can state that each possibility is just an option, and that no one possibility is "right."

Teach a new technique

At the next level down the continuum, you teach clients a new technique or strategy. You could teach a progressive relaxation exercise, a format for delivering an "I-message," a process for visualization and affirmation, or a problem-solving technique. These are just a few examples.

When you coach at this level, be careful. When you teach a technique, many clients will assume that you've just given them the "right" answer. It's hard for people to receive instruction as just one possibility.

Offer an option

Sometimes you can empower clients by moving along to the next level on the coaching continuum and offering just one option. For example: "I notice that you drink a lot more than I do and more than most people I know. I'm wondering if this is a problem for you, and if you would like to set up a structure for having a wonderful life while drinking less."

The same problem can occur when you offer an option as when you teach a technique. Clients can easily hear this option as *the* thing for them to do.

However, generating one possibility can sometimes work well, as long as clients hold it as a genuine offer and invitation—and when they feel comfortable saying no to the option. You can even make this an explicit request: "Please don't hear this idea as a direction or something you *should* do. What I'm presenting is just an option that you can choose to accept or not."

An advantage of presenting an option is that it can provide the client with something to argue against. For example, one of my clients was complaining about his wife. So I said, "Well, maybe you ought to just divorce her." This brought an immediate reaction from him and a long list of ways in which he could solve this problem without anything nearly as drastic as divorce.

Give advice

I do not consider the last three levels on this continuum (giving advice, giving advice by sharing or questioning, and giving *the* answer) to be a part of coaching. Before you give advice, consider the distinction between coaching and advising. I have heard a lot of people say they are coaching someone when they are really giving him advice. I claim that giving advice and coaching are two entirely different ways of being with people.

The distinction between coaching and advising does not exist in the dictionary. From my point of view, when you give advice, you are then consulting, not coaching.

Giving advice is common and can be useful. And, I do not intend to give advice when I coach people. Dwelling on the non-directive levels of the coaching continuum is so valuable that this is how I want to be with people.

A basic assumption of life coaches is that when there really is a clear answer, people will probably discover it for themselves and this discovery is facilitated through the process of coaching. Giving advice goes directly against this assumption. For clients, there's a clear difference between self-discovery and taking on someone else's idea, even if it's a great idea. Self-discovery reinforces the benefits of choice, commitment, and responsibility—the kinds of processes that are most likely to help people create the life of their dreams. Coaching assists people to maintain an internal locus of control. Advice, even great advice, reinforces an external locus of control.

CONSIDER THE CASE AGAINST ADVICE

Clients want advice, and we're often pulled to give it. We live in a culture that is permeated with advice. People often ask for advice even though they don't want to follow it—perhaps *especially* when they don't want to follow it. They might just want to be polite or to make conversation.

Advice reinforces the coach's brilliance, not the client's. When a client presents a problem, I could say, "This is a pretty straight-forward issue, one I deal with all the time, and here's how to solve it." The danger is that my client may then leave the coaching session saying to herself, "Boy, I sure have a brilliant coach." That's not what I want. I want the client to leave saying, "Boy, am I ever smart—I just came up with a brilliant solution."

I see several other problems with advice, including the following:

- Advice can fail.
- Advice can insult people by implying that they are incapable of handling their own problems.
- Advice can be presumptuous: I can offer advice without really knowing the client well or knowing the full extent of the client's problem.
- Advice can be limiting by pointing in one direction toward only one solution.

BREAK THE ADVICE HABIT

Giving advice can be an unconscious habit for us. If it is, we can apply several strategies to change it:

- Develop skills to replace advice giving, including full listening, giving possibilities, and other activities on the higher end of the coaching continuum.
- When meeting with clients, announce your intention to avoid advice. Ask clients to remind you of your intention.
- Bracket advice. Point out when you're about to give advice and state that for the moment you are no longer coaching.

- Ask clients how they feel about getting advice before you give it.

- Monitor how often you give advice. Ask others to help you monitor this behavior. Most behaviors tend to change in the direction of our intention when we monitor them.

- Start a support group for people who want to stop giving advice. Present your problem with advice to the group—and accept no advice about how to solve it.

- Pre-answer objections to your strategy of not giving advice: "Please don't be insulted that I don't offer advice. I intend this to be a huge compliment. If I withhold my advice, you can think more deeply and creatively and come up with answers that are much better than mine."

RESPOND TO REQUESTS FOR ADVICE

Suppose that you are in a life coaching interaction, perhaps with a client that you've been meeting with for months. The client says, "Look, I just want some advice here. I don't know whether to stay with my husband or leave my husband. Give me some advice." Or, "I don't know whether to buy a new house or stay in my apartment. Can you give me some advice?" Or, "I don't know whether to quit my job or not. I want to know your point of view because you know me so well."

I've stated several times that life coaching is about following the client's direction and assisting clients to get what they want. That can be tough when what they want is advice.

Even when clients make a direct request for advice, you have many options:

- *Feed back the dilemma*: "So you're unclear about whether to leave him or stay married. Is that right?" When they hear the request for advice rephrased in this way, clients will often continue reflecting on the problem. They might even solve the problem then and there.

- *Talk about the problems with advice.* Remind clients that although you might have a lot of advice on the tip of your tongue, you don't think that advice is empowering. Talk about the purpose of coaching as assisting clients to invent their own ideas and to experience the joy of creating their own solutions.

- *Ask clients to create their own advice:* "If your best friend had a similar problem, what advice would you offer?"

- *Ask clients to assume that there's a part of themselves that is brilliant and creative.* Then set up an exercise where clients role-play talking to that brilliant part of themselves.

AND, SOMETIMES, JUST GIVE ADVICE

After you've considered all the alternatives to advice, sometimes you might just choose to give advice. Though it's not life coaching, advice can be appropriate and useful.

Advice can even inspire people to keep thinking and inventing. For example, you say, "Look, I don't think you should buy a house. Renting is much cheaper." Faced with such blunt advice, your client might respond, "Even if it is cheaper to rent, I just want a house of my own. I've always wanted my own place so that I can fix it up and have a permanent garden." Bumping up against your advice has just moved the client forward.

What I've given you in the last few pages is just a bunch of advice about advice. In summary, my message is not an absolute directive to avoid advice but rather a caution to beware of it.

Give advice by sharing or questioning

You can advise clients in a way that's even more subtle than giving direct advice—and perhaps even manipulative. This is advising by sharing or asking a question. Consider these examples:

- "This is what I did in a similar situation…"

- "Another client had a similar situation and here's what he did…"
- "Well, you know, I would never tell you what to do, but let me tell you what my Aunt Bertha did…"
- "I would never give you advice, but let me ask you, have you ever considered…?"

In addition to all the disadvantages of giving advice mentioned earlier, this method of giving advice makes it harder for your client to detect and reject the advice.

Give the *answer*

At the end of the continuum exists a level even less effective than advice. At this level, you just give the "right" answer:

- "I see only one option for you, and that is…"
- "Listen up, because here's what you need to do…"
- "I know only one thing to tell you, and that's…"

As I mentioned earlier, we can sometimes give advice that moves clients to create their own options. When we give *the* answer, it's hard for clients to create much of anything. At this point we've descended to a level that's the polar opposite of full listening. This puts us well outside the realm of coaching.

Choose your place on the continuum

At a given moment, you and your clients are free to participate at any level of the coaching continuum.

Ask clients to help you choose

One option is to let clients choose the level where they feel most effective. To assist them in making that choice, you can briefly review some levels of the continuum: "One of the things I could do today is give you a few options. Or, I could just listen fully to help you facilitate your thinking." In effect, you give clients a menu and let them "order" the kind of interaction they want.

Ask for feedback

Once in a while, ask for feedback about the level of your interaction: "My intention is not to direct you. Do you think I have been?" You can repeat your commitment to choose a level on the continuum that empowers the client and then periodically check out how you are doing.

Go for multiple action plans (MAPs)

When I move up and down the coaching continuum, I intend for the client to leave the session with many solutions to her problem or many ways to reach her goal. This is freedom. One solution, one answer is not freedom.

If we are confident that we have the answer, we often stop searching for more. Circumstances of life do not always conform to our plans. It is fairly common to run into setbacks and unforeseen barriers. With no alternative plans, we can become stuck and disappointed. Having to start all over and make a new plan can rob us of our enthusiasm. Having just one path to reach a goal is like having only one tool to do a job. It's not very effective.

I was fixing a leak in my upstairs bathroom and was pretty sure I knew which wrench I needed. So I went down to the basement, picked the right wrench out of my toolbox, and climbed back up the two flights of stairs. I soon discovered that I needed a different wrench. So I went back downstairs, got the wrench I needed, and returned to complete the work. Well, you can probably guess what happened next. Wrong wrench again. When I went downstairs for the third time, I just brought up the whole toolbox. And I was glad I did.

After we assist our clients to determine what they want, our job is to help them create multiple actions plans (MAPs) to achieve their goals and manifest their dreams. It is risky to embark on a journey and have only one set of directions. If we give advice, it is a lot like giving directions to a lost traveler. "Oh, the interstate? Sure. Go back five miles to the big red barn. Take the next right and follow the winding road. Be sure to stay to the left. There's a pond on the right. Turn left on the second road after the pond and it will turn into a paved road. At the four-way stop..." The problem with directions (or one answer) is that if something goes wrong, it is difficult to find your way.

Instead of our clients setting out with one set of directions, we can assist them to design MAPs. If they miss a turn, have to take a detour, or get lost, they can check their map for another route and get back on track.

Creating MAPs involves staying in an inquiry and pushing beyond the first few answers. Sometimes it is after you're pretty sure that all the good ones have been thought of that a great new idea shows up.

One way to stay in the inquiry is to offer to take turns with your client. First, they can think of an idea and then it is your turn to think of a new possibility.

Generating new solutions and answers is a lot like brainstorming. The idea is to be wild and crazy and go for quantity. After clients think of lots of possibilities, they can start to evaluate and choose the ones that they want to keep. Then you can facilitate developing those ideas in more detail.

Stay flexible

If it seems to you that your client is not being empowered or energized, then change the approach and switch to a different level. Descending to the more directive levels of the continuum can serve clients, so long as you're careful and do it consciously.

When I'm in doubt about which level to occupy, I return to the miracle of life coaching—that clients are fully capable of creating a wonderful life. Remembering this helps me choose, moment by moment, an effective place along the continuum.

Chapter Four
Enhancing Your Skills

Assisting clients to discover their passion

We can learn to be with people so that, in a short time, they wake up to what really turns them on. Then we can encourage them to follow the path of their passion and trust that this will carry them to a wonderful life.

This conversation about passion is one of the most valuable benefits you can offer to clients. Each of the following suggestions can help you and your clients move into that conversation with ease.

Presume passion

To begin, I assume that people are passionate about something and that my job is to help them discover that passion, whatever it is. I have yet to meet anyone who has no passion. I have yet to meet anyone who wants nothing. What I do find is that people often lack the opportunity to explore new possibilities and desires. Life coaching constantly gives people that opportunity.

One of the foundations of life coaching is seeing each client as brilliant and then listening for their brilliance. Likewise, if you keep listening to people with the presumption that they're passionate about something, they will likely find it. Once their passion is uncovered and supported, clients' lives can transform magically.

Listen fully

In assisting people to get in touch with their passion, full listening is the technique that I apply more than any other. When people receive the gift of full listening, they start to speak freely about their upsets, their secrets, their anger, their sadness, their embarrassment—and then their passions. Full listening allows people to get past the obstacles to their creativity and to invent goals they care about deeply.

When you listen fully, you assist people to move from the disappointments of the past to the joys of the present moment and to the creative possibilities for the future. When you listen fully, boredom can blossom into an inspiring passion.

Listen fully and affirm

In addition to listening fully, we can notice when clients speak their dreams for the future. We can then point out those dreams and reinforce them. Every time a goal falls out of a client's mouth, we can affirm that goal.

Whenever I affirm a goal, I am, in a sense, directing the coaching conversation, and subtly "steering the show." But I'm steering in a way that's consistent with my role as a coach, which is to uncover clients' passion and unlock their brilliance.

I don't think we can motivate employees about work, or motivate children about school, or motivate clients about life. What we can do is look to see when people become passionate, motivated, and turned on, and then invite them to speak more about that—whatever it is.

Feed back clients' passions and goals

As a life coach, I become a filter for my clients as they speak. I can hear their complaints and absorb those. I can hear about their embarrassments and absorb them. I can hear their upsets and their secrets and absorb those also. Then, when I hear their passions, I can choose to feed those back: "So you want to travel more?" Or, "So one of the things you really want is to get along better with that spouse of yours." Or, "I hear you saying that you really want to make some major changes in your health habits."

When I respond in this way, clients usually start going into more detail about what they want. And if we stay in that inquiry, people can directly contact their passion. When offered in an effective way, feedback acts like a magnet that draws people into creating their future.

Every time a client goes beyond a general statement of their passion and speaks a more specific goal, you can feed back that goal with affirmation. As clients gain clarity about that they want and start articulating it, you can build on what they say. What will come with your listening, affirmation, and feedback is a more fully developed goal that translates into passion.

Open up an inquiry

The following questions are a huge gift we can give our clients: *What do you want? What are you interested in? What do you do for fun? What brings you joy? What are your plans, dreams, hopes, and wishes? What would you like to have happen in your life next year? What would you like next month? What would you like right now?* Clients' answers might be about careers, relationships, kids, cars, fly-fishing, or anything else.

By asking questions, you are directing the client's conversation instead of following the client's lead. This is why you want to be cautious and thoughtful as you ask these questions. Questions can function like a condiment when the main course of the coaching menu is full listening, complete affirmation, and feeding back the client's celebrations, desires, and action plans.

When asking questions, have them all be variations of "What do you want?" "When do you want it?" "With whom do you want it?" "Where do you want it?"

Focus on being

Coaches assist their clients to get more of whatever they want in all areas of life. Most of the time, clients will focus on what they want to have and what they want to do. What's often missing is the critical issue of who they want to be. It is from this domain that passion often arises.

The domain of being includes values, beliefs, and attitudes. The attributes a person chooses to adopt in the domain of being have a significant influence over what they end up having and doing. For example, a person who values being willing to take risks will have a more adventurous life than someone who values safety so much that he is fearful of new experiences. Given the impact that ways of being have on the quality of people's lives, it makes sense for coaches to encourage their clients to devote some time and energy to determining who they want to be.

People get to choose who they want to be without much interference from the outside. They have less control in the domain of doing because sometimes what they do is influenced by others, or by circumstances outside of their control. And people have even less control in the domain of having because what they have is even more dramatically influenced by external circumstances. Their "being" is more of an internal matter, and that is where they have the most control.

Probably the easiest and most effective way to have clients explore the domain of being is to simply ask them to develop a written set of values. They can choose who they want to be in life in general, and they can also choose who they want to be in specific situations and relationships. For example, if your client is going to give a presentation to a group, you can ask her to consider who she wants to be while she is presenting. She might choose to be light and humorous or serious and formal. Her way of being will likely have as much of an impact, or even more, than the content she chooses to deliver. You can ask your clients who they want to be as parents, spouses, children, friends, employees, employers, captains of their bowling teams, or as participants in any relationships they have in their lives.

The advantage of thoughtfully choosing who they want to be and having a well-defined set of values is that clients then have a reference that allows them to align their behaviors with their chosen ways of being and values. They can consult their values whenever they are confused about their passion. Whether it's a major decision like choosing a career or a marriage, or a minor decision like what to have for dinner or which TV show to watch, their values and ways of being can supply guidelines to help them get in touch with their passion and make choices.

Create scenarios

When I assist people to create their future, I use a lot of "what if" questions. This is a great way to uncover peoples' passion and create scenarios that unleash their creativity. Some examples are:

- *What if you had all the money you ever wanted? Then what would you do with your life?* You can vary this question in many ways, and I think the more specifically you set up the scenario, the more powerful the question can be. Instead of asking, "What if you had all the money you ever wanted?" you could ask, "What if you had three million dollars? Thirty thousand dollars? Three thousand more dollars? Three hundred more dollars?" For many people, three million dollars is so much money that they can't relate to it. But they might get to their passion if you ask them about thirty thousand or three thousand dollars instead. You could also ask, "What if you lost your job and got a severance package that included two years of your current salary?"
- *What if your family would support anything you chose to do? What would you do then?* Many people see their loved ones as obstacles to creating a new future. When clients begin to remove that obstacle—even if only in their imagination—they can take the lid off their creativity.
- *What if you had no family members to consider when making plans for the future?* If clients are married or have children, they can imagine that they are single and childless instead. For a variation on

this theme, ask, "What if none of your relatives lived near you and you could move anywhere in the world without disappointing your family? Where would you live and what would you do?"

- *What if you had three days with nothing to do—no family to care for, no job responsibilities, and no house maintenance? What would you do with your time?* Play with extending the time from three days to one month, one year, five years, and even more.

- *What if you found a magic lantern, rubbed it, and awakened a genie who could grant you five wishes—anything you ask for?* This is the stuff of fairy tales, and your clients may respond to it and discover their passions.

People can use money, marriage, children, career, and many other circumstances as obstacles to living the life of their dreams. We can help clients transcend this self-limiting practice. We can ask "what if" questions to start moving people toward their passion.

Write down clients' passions

As your client responds to questions, you can write down his answers in the form of goals. Grab a stack of 3×5 cards, and write one goal per card. Your client can think more creatively when he is not distracted by the writing process. Later, he can sort through the cards, arrange them in different categories, and set priorities. As you are writing your client's goals, you will often see a gleam in his eyes. That's when you know he is beginning to talk about his passion.

After he is done brainstorming his passions and goals, read what you've written out loud. Often this practice inspires your client to brainstorm about even more passions and goals.

Life coaching is a profession based on giving people some of the biggest gifts they will ever receive. And one of those gifts is their documented speaking—a visible record of his hopes, wishes, and dreams.

Ask clients to write about their passions and dreams

When we ask people what they're passionate about, they might go blank and just say, "I don't know." But if you ask them to write down their passions, the same people can often generate dozens of ideas.

Again, 3×5 cards work well for this purpose. Ask your client to write down one goal per card. Give her permission to generate piles and piles of cards—spontaneously, almost thoughtlessly. Later, she can sort through the piles and choose ideas that she can turn into more concrete plans.

When somebody says, "I don't know," you can also say, "Well, I know you don't know, but if you *did* know, what would you want? Just pretend you know and write down the first thing that pops into your head."

Suspend judgment

Sometimes helping people discover their passion calls for coaches to suspend judgment about the client's initial path. Suppose a client says that his passion is fly-fishing. My first reaction as a coach may be to think, "Wake up and smell the roses, there's a whole lot more to life than that." Instead, I could say, "Okay. So how can you get more fly-fishing in your life? How can you live so that you wake up every day with the excitement that you bring to fly fishing?"

I could also ask, "What is it about fly-fishing that you like?" The client answers, "Being outside." Now I can help him explore how he can live a life that allows him to be outside every day. Staying in the inquiry about fly-fishing could lead the client to a new career.

Ask for complaints

Another option is to ask about the client's complaints and then turn those complaints into goals. If the client complains that his life is boring, you now know that one of his goals is to make his life exciting.

When clients say what they don't want, you can then feed back what they *do* want. Suppose that your client says, "I don't want to get up every morning and rush off to work." You can say, "So what you want to do is get up leisurely in the morning?" Another client says, "I don't want to go home and have my kids be upset with me." You can say, "I got it—you want happy kids when you go home?"

When you restate the client's complaints as goals or passions, you might miss sometimes. That's okay. Ask clients whether you're accurately stating what they want. In the process of giving you feedback, they'll start to clarify their passions.

Review the past

Another way you can assist people to discover their passions for the future is to see what they've been passionate about or excelled at in the past. Ask them to make a list of what they've done well in the past or what their aims were when they graduated from high school. Many people's passions fade as they get older, but they frequently have memories of times when they *were* passionate. Assist them to look back and bring those passions forward.

Invite people to discharge emotion about thwarted plans

Thwarted plans often stop people from realizing their passion. When they're young, people often want something passionately. Perhaps they went all out for that passion and they lost. They didn't get the dream job, or the house, or the relationship they wanted. They just felt defeated.

To assist these people to become passionate again, you can invite them to release their pent-up or hidden emotions about their thwarted plans. Let them speak about it. Let them cry and rage about it. If their passion was thwarted, they might not be willing or able to uncover that passion again until they release all their upset feelings about it. As a matter of fact, people probably won't discharge about this unless they get some encouragement. Offering encouragement to discharge emotion is an important service you can provide.

Knowing your client

As you get to know more and more details about your clients' lives, your relationships with them will become deeper and more intimate. The more you know about all of the various relationships in their lives and the major events that have influenced them, the better you will be able to facilitate their progress in reaching their goals.

Even though getting to know your clients may sound like something that should be done at the beginning of the coaching relationship, it can be valuable at any time. Here are two exercises to help you get to know your clients better. With new clients, I recommend you do these in the first few sessions. If that opportunity has already past, you can do them whenever you think it makes sense.

Have your client draw a relationship map

The first exercise involves asking each of your clients to draw a relationship map. As they draw their map, they can describe what they are doing and you can draw a similar map. Or when they complete their relationship map, they can send you a copy.

Have clients start by putting their name in the middle of the page. Then they can draw geometric shapes to represent all the different people in their lives. Circles can represent family members, triangles can represent friends, squares can represent work relationships, and diamonds can represent others. They can write the name of a person inside each of the shapes.

Ask your clients to represent how frequently they are in contact with each person by how near or far they draw each shape from their name. If they are in frequent contact, they can draw that person's shape fairly close to their name. If they contact the person rarely, they can draw the shape farther away from their name.

Then ask your clients to represent how close they feel to each person by drawing lines of various thickness between their name and the shape representing each person. The more intimate the relationship, the thicker the line. So, for example, the figure representing a colleague who your client sees every day at work but doesn't like very much will be very close to your client's name with a very thin line. Conversely, your client might have an old friend who he contacts only every few years, but with whom he feels very close. This person's shape will be far from your client's name with a thick connecting line.

Use five-year review

The second exercise invites your clients to review their entire lives in five-year increments. Ask clients to write down both the highlights and lowlights of every five-year period from when they were born to the present. If one year was particularly eventful, your client can bracket out that year and log the occurrences in it. Reviewing these major life events with a client might just take a few minutes. If your client has a high level of interest and perceives a lot of value in the exercise, the review could endure over several sessions and could take hours.

These two exercises not only help you get to know your clients better, they also assist your clients to acknowledge and evaluate their relationships and their histories. While doing these exercises, it is possible that clients will become aware of changes they want to make and invent some new goals for their futures.

Evaluating your life coaching

One path to greater effectiveness, satisfaction, and enjoyment of life coaching is through continuous self-evaluation. Coaches can do the same thing they ask clients to do by regularly reflecting on their performance and setting goals to enhance their skills.

The words "inspect" and "respect" come from the Latin words "inspectus" and "respectus" which mean "to look back." This points to the possibility that inspecting something is a form of respecting it. Conversely, it can be argued that what is not inspected is not respected.

Trying to improve our effectiveness as coaches without periodic evaluation is like trying to improve our ability as marksmen while we are blindfolded. Without knowing if we are hitting the mark, it is impossible to make corrections and improve.

Listed below are several ways to evaluate your performance. With evaluations, you can continually improve and become an even better coach.

Monitor in the moment and evaluate afterwards

During a session, skilled coaches focus primarily on doing whatever is appropriate to forward the client's agenda. At the same time, they lightly monitor their performance so they can evaluate it later. Paying too much attention during sessions to the kind of job you are doing takes the focus away from clients and can compromise your effectiveness. Focusing primarily on clients while limiting focus on your own performance becomes natural with just a little practice.

I love the country western song that counsels to not count your money while you're sitting at the table, since "there'll be time enough for counting when the dealin's done." I use that line as a reminder to assess my coaching *after* the session. Too much self-evaluation during the session often results in undue pressure. When I start worrying about my performance, I can become self-conscious and lose sight of my primary purpose. During the session, I think it's more powerful to focus on what the client is getting, not on how well I'm doing.

Review your sessions with colleagues

I review well over half of my coaching calls with another life coach. I think it would be ideal to do this for every session.

When reviewing a coaching session, you can look to see where you got stuck and what you might do differently in the future. Also, look for moments that are worth celebrating. This process of regularly getting coaching about your coaching can quickly take you to new levels of competence.

Tape your sessions

You can use technology as an evaluation tool. Ask clients for permission to either audiotape or videotape sessions. You can evaluate and critique yourself as you listen to the tape. You can also share these tapes with other coaches and ask them for their feedback. If you plan to share the tapes with other professionals, it's essential to get your client's permission.

Notice verbal and non-verbal cues

One way to assess the effectiveness of your coaching is to listen for the results that clients report. When coaching makes a difference, you'll often hear clients say that their lives are thriving and that they're getting more of what they want. Another sign that the coaching is working is that clients come to sessions with full agendas and a lot to say.

When you meet in person, observe non-verbal cues. If you are conducting sessions on the telephone, voice tone and tempo can often give you much of the same feedback as non-verbal language. Notice whether clients light up when they first see you. Observe whether they stay attentive and alert during sessions. See if they seem more animated at the end of a session than at the beginning. Notice whether clients honor the coaching relationship by being on time for sessions, completing assignments, giving you referrals, and making timely payments. I don't want a client to view life coaching as a chance for some informal, friendly conversation. Instead, I want a client with a real appetite and demand for coaching and for big changes in her life. I want someone who's rolled up her sleeves and is sitting on the edge of her chair, pen in hand, taking copious notes. I want a client who's ready for something big to happen in her life. Clients usually communicate this level of intensity with their body language as well as with their words.

Request verbal evaluations

At the end of a session, you can ask the client for a review of the coaching. You might say, "I am very committed to having this be powerful and effective for you. How was it? Were you disappointed about anything that I said or did today? And is there anything about today's session that worked particularly well?" As clients respond, listen, take detailed notes, and start forming your intentions about any changes you want to make.

Complete written self-evaluations

Periodically, you can complete a written evaluation of your performance as a life coach. After completing a self-evaluation, you can design and implement action plans to improve current limitations and enhance your strengths and what is already working well. Here are some statements to consider when evaluating yourself.

- I evaluate my life coaching skills on a regular basis.
- I periodically get feedback from each of my clients.

- I clearly distinguish and acknowledge what I do well as a life coach.
- I clearly distinguish and acknowledge my current limitations and ways that I could improve my life coaching.
- I take effective notes during my conversations.
- I prepare for every call and have topics to recommend.
- I review every call and enter notes for future conversations.
- My clients leave each session with assignments they have agreed to complete.
- I offer my clients alternative ways to communicate (in person, voicemail, e-mail, fax).
- I offer my clients a variety of flexible options regarding the frequency of our sessions. (For example, there may be times when daily check-ins would be useful, and there might be other times when it is appropriate to take a vacation break.)
- I've suggested various lengths of time for conversations with clients, from a quick five-minute check-in to a two-day strategic life-planning retreat. During a typical session, I pay attention to how much time I spend listening and how much time I spend speaking.
- My coaching sessions are balanced with levity and fun.
- I have a written contract with each of my clients defining his commitments and my commitments. I have thoughtfully reviewed this contract within the last six months.
- I keep all the agreements I make with my clients and, when necessary, I renegotiate them in a timely way.
- I hold my clients accountable to the agreements they make with me.
- I regularly discuss coaching issues with other life coaches.
- I share my best thinking with my clients without giving advice.
- I have a professional development plan, and am I implementing that plan.
- I trust my clients' desires, innate intelligence, intuition, ability, and creativity. I treat them consistently knowing that genius lives within them, and my role is to help them uncover it.
- I grant my clients their reality. I make them "right."

- I periodically review my clients' goals, commitments, and promises with them.
- I use notes and other ways to remind myself to think about each of my clients every day.

Request written evaluations from your clients

Consider asking for periodic written evaluations from your clients. Here are some possible questions. Use them to help you design your own questionnaire. Reviewing your evaluation form periodically helps you ensure that it continues to be useful and fit for you and your clients.

- Have I been giving you advice instead of coaching?
- Would you prefer I speak more or listen more in our sessions?
- Could I make the coaching more effective by offering to meet with you at different times?
- Would you like to use e-mail, faxes, or voice mail as part of our work?
- Would you prefer to meet more or less frequently?
- In our coaching relationship, describe specifically what is working.
- In our coaching relationship, describe specifically what can be improved.
- What specific changes have you made that have improved the quality of your personal life?
- What specific changes have you made that have improved the quality of your professional life?
- What have I done that has benefited you the most?
- What have I done that has disappointed you the most?
- While working with me, what have you done that are you most proud of?
- While working with me, what have you done that are you most disappointed in?
- This relationship is designed to produce life-changing results. To what degree are we succeeding?

Using six types of conversation

It's useful to remember how many different ways we can be in conversation with each other. Below are six types of conversation. Some of these types of conversations are more useful than others in the life coaching relationship.

- Sharing
- Debriefing
- Clearing
- Discussion and debate
- Teaching
- Coaching

Sharing

Sharing is a process whereby the speaker communicates the essence of who she is, what she is thinking, and how she is feeling at the moment. This is the kernel—the heart of the matter—a quick snapshot provided in just a few minutes.

Sharing might sound like this:

"Life's tough these days. I've really been having problems with my boss, and my teenage daughter is rebellious. I wish I had more time to deal with these problems."

"I really enjoyed the trip that I just took to San Francisco. We had a great time just visiting with people and exploring the city. In general, life is just such a celebration recently."

"I'm worried about my health. My doctor said that I need to come in for three difficult tests, and I'm scared. I so love being active, and I don't want anything to get in the way of that."

"I just got a $3,000 raise, and I was really surprised. I feel so pleased that my hard work has been recognized. Now I'm starting to think about what to do with the extra money."

One way to be a powerful life coach is to demonstrate and ask for sharing. By sharing, I mean speaking deeply, authentically, and comprehensively about where you are in the present moment. You and your clients can learn to speak soulfully from the depths of your being about who you are in the moment. This is a sacred way to be with each other, and it's unusual.

Many people find sharing difficult to do at first. When people ask, "How are you?", many just give a brief, superficial reply ("Just fine, thanks"). Other people habitually go into a long "weather report" full of unrelated details. Both responses can conceal who we really are in the moment.

When we share, we don't always have to reveal deep, dark secrets. Nor is releasing emotion always necessary. The main idea is to let people know how we are in a way that they didn't know a couple of minutes earlier. This kind of speaking is deeply felt, soulful, sincere, candid, and to the point. When someone tells the truth about how they are and does it briefly and deeply, all the world's jabber stops for a moment. Powerful sharing moves us deeply and alters the subsequent conversation. Sharing can turn things around in the world.

As a life coach, you can model this kind of speaking and ask for it from your clients. One option is to start most coaching sessions by asking your clients to share. If clients respond instead with their agenda for the session, you can describe sharing in more detail, demonstrate it, and ask again for them to share.

What you can bring to a client's sharing is your full, committed, and heartfelt listening. This is also a unique and difficult response. When people share, we're often tempted to give advice, launch a discussion, or "piggyback" on their comments by relating our own experience ("You know, the same thing happened to me; let me tell you about it....") As recipients of someone else's sharing, our job is to postpone our own response and simply receive.

We can even do others a favor when we ask them to receive in this way: "Please don't give me any advice about this. You don't have to make any suggestions or do any problem-solving. I just want you to listen. I just want to share."

Debriefing

Another service you can provide as a life coach is time for people to debrief.

Debriefing is different from sharing. While sharing is about who clients are *being* in the moment, debriefing is a list of what clients have been *doing* in the last few days or weeks. When clients debrief, they give you a detailed report. Similar to a newspaper article, debriefing relates the breaking events in the client's recent past and answers the "who, what, where, when, and how" questions.

Sharing offers up a taste of how clients are in the moment; debriefing serves up the "whole enchilada"—a long list of what they've done and felt since you last saw them.

When I debrief, my coach usually doesn't say much. Instead, I might verbally review a two- or three-day period in 10 to 20 minutes or so. And through this speaking, I can get clean and clear.

Clients can experience similar benefits. More specifically, they can:

- Learn from their recent history by talking about what worked and what didn't work. With that insight, they're more likely to repeat what *does* work.
- Forgive their mistakes, celebrate their successes, and then release the past. Debriefing can include all of these elements.
- Set goals. As the client reviews the last few days, he might realize what he wants to change.

As a coach, you also gain a lot from the client's conscious review of recent events. For instance, you become very informed about the client. You can also start to notice patterns in your client's thinking and behavior. If you spot a recurring mistake or recurring success in the client's life, those are more details for your data bank and more sources of powerful feedback that you can later share with your client.

Encourage clients to debrief regularly with a variety of people in a variety of ways. One way to sell them on the value of this tool is to first get them hooked on debriefing with you. Clients can also debrief with other significant people in their lives. They can debrief privately through writing in a journal, speaking into a tape recorder, or simply by talking out loud to themselves. You can suggest that clients commit to this new behavior and monitor how often they debrief on their own, just as you would assist them to acquire any other habit.

Please bring debriefing into your coaching and into your life. If it gives you half as much benefit as it gives me, then it's a habit well worth gaining.

Clearing

Another form of a life coaching conversation with a unique purpose is clearing. When clients clear, they vent feelings. Clearing is pure emotional release where a person just aims to speak about a topic until he "gets it off his chest."

Clearing differs from both sharing and debriefing. Sharing is soulful and *brief* speaking. In contrast, clearing is most effective for clients when we place no time limits on their speaking. And, unlike debriefing, clearing does not result in a detailed review of recent events in the client's life. When clearing, clients could focus on a single event and their emotional response to it.

Clearing is a powerful form of conversation, and there is much you can do to facilitate it. For related suggestions, see "Handling emotions" in the next chapter.

Discussion and debate

Discussion and debate are probably the dominant forms of conversation in our society, and they take place in large groups, small groups, or even dyads. This type of conversation does not have much place in most life coaching. Discussion and debate occur when people express their views about topics. Sometimes people stick to one topic (which is unusual) and create a new idea from different points of view.

Discussion and debate can both be wonderful ways to promote learning. That learning happens when we see a subject from many different sides. We can then come away with a point of view that's larger than what any one person first brought to the conversation.

Discussion and debate work best when people share the conversation space and everyone's brilliance comes into the arena. One way to see that the space is being shared is to ensure that everyone has about the same amount of time to speak his point of view on the topic.

Even when people use that time to explain that they don't have a point of view, this contributes to the group process. People who declare that they don't have a stand on a particular issue can be more open-minded and bring a fresh perspective to the conversation. Also, they demonstrate that it's okay not to have a point of view, and that there's no need to adopt one immediately.

Teaching

Another way that we can be in conversation with each other is teaching. Teaching occurs when somebody says, "I know something that you may not know, and I'd like to share it with you." When others want to learn from this person, they often listen intently, take notes, search to understand, and ask questions about the information until they're clear. Sometimes in a teaching environment, debate and discussion occur. And, sometimes in an unusual teaching environment, sharing even occurs.

I recommend that you minimize the amount of teaching you do in a coaching relationship. Teaching is more likely to be the job of a consultant. Even when you know a lot about the subject that's on the table during a coaching session, you're there to assist people to get in touch with their brilliance. That's far less likely to happen when you use the type of conversation that we call teaching.

Coaching

There's one more unique and distinct way that we can be in conversation with each other, and that's coaching. This type of conversation takes place when people explore what they want in the future and choose ways to attain it—without getting advice.

In the context of a coaching relationship, you do many different things with clients: exploring, problem solving, creative thinking, generating lots of options (some that contradict), and experimenting with new strategies and techniques. And sometimes coaching just means listening fully and occasionally feeding back what you hear (particularly what we hear about the client's celebrations, dreams, and action plans). Throughout this activity, the client's purpose is to generate his next new action—usually that does not happen in sharing, debriefing, discussion, debate, or teaching.

Use one type of conversation at a time

Consider keeping each type of conversation separate, at least in the beginning of a coaching relationship. That way, for example, your clients' sharing won't get coached, and their debriefing won't get discussed and debated. To experience the full power of any type of conversation, choose it consciously.

Maintaining appropriate balance in the life coaching relationship

The life coaching relationship is intentionally out of balance in terms of intimacy. The client purposely does most of the talking, and therefore most of the self-revelation, struggling, and self-examination. As a coach, you might do a little of that for yourself as a model to the client, but you are primarily there to facilitate a transformational process for someone else.

This lack of balance in the life coaching relationship happens by design and creates value for the client. Our clients have few people in their lives who are as willing to assist them as we are.

Most other kinds of helping relationships are also out of balance in this way, no matter whether it involves a priest, counselor, physician, or consultant. And although helping relationships are usually out of balance to some degree, there are ways that you can enhance the coaching relationship by bringing it into more balance.

Share

By making time for your own sharing and doing this regularly, you can match some of the client's vulnerability with your authenticity. Learning to share briefly and deeply can help you achieve some level of balance in a way that doesn't take too much time.

Carefully offer examples from your own life

When I coach, I only rarely illustrate a point or explain an option by giving an example from my own life. This is a conscious choice on my part. In giving examples, it's too easy for me to take the floor and steer the conversation away from the client. Also, when listening to my examples, clients might start thinking that I'm brilliant and really have my life together and that the way to solve their problem is to do it the way I did it in my example. That's not what I want. Instead, I want people to generate their own options, create their own solutions, and leave a coaching session thinking that *they* are brilliant and have *their* lives together.

I know life coaches who routinely give examples from their own lives, and this seems to work. My suggestion is that when you bring your own examples to life coaching, that you do so consciously, carefully, and briefly.

Speak about yourself in a contributing way

When you share or debrief during a coaching session, you can speak about your goals and achievements in a way that contributes to your client and does not sound like bragging.

To begin, ask that your client focus primarily on your excitement and your joy about your life, not on your specific accomplishments. You can even make a request such as, "I want to tell you a little about what's been happening with me, and I don't want to sound pompous or grandiose. Mainly, I'm just thrilled about the wonderful life I get to live, and my purpose is to hold out the possibility that any of us can create the life of our dreams."

Also, give the client an accurate picture of your accomplishments to avoid sounding like you're boasting. For example, "One of my goals is to raise $100 million to end world hunger, and I am not doing this alone. Many people have taken on this goal with me." When talking about a long-term project, speak about results to date and how far you have yet to go.

Nurture yourself

Please take time to nurture yourself. When you do, you have more to offer clients. Discover ways to balance your life so that you are receiving as much nurturing outside of your coaching relationships as you are giving to them. Do whatever fills you up, whether that is walking in the woods, spending time by the ocean, going to a therapist, getting a massage, sitting in a hot tub, or going to church.

In particular, consider two more options for nurturing yourself. One is to have your own life coach and experience the power of life coaching for yourself. The other is to avoid working too much. I have yet to meet anybody who is energetic enough to do 40 hours a week of life coaching. To do this work, you might need to devote almost half of the week to just keeping yourself clear.

Asking questions cautiously

Questions are often very valuable. As a life coach, I sometimes ask questions to gently guide the conversation toward the goals my client has said that she wants to achieve and how she might achieve those goals. This is one way to prevent clients from spending an entire session just shooting the breeze.

I also think that questions have serious potential drawbacks. By their nature, questions steer a conversation in a certain direction, and it may not be the direction that a client wants to go. Few clients are assertive enough to say, "I don't want to answer that question right now." Questions are directive, and I'd like coaching to remain non-directive and client-centered.

In addition, questions can contain hidden statements ("Don't you see that this is the most powerful option?") or implicit advice ("I don't want to tell you what to do, but wouldn't it be better to just get divorced?").

We can become more aware of our habit of asking questions unconsciously. Then we can apply the following strategies so that our coaching contains fewer and more powerful questions.

Stop asking questions

Promise yourself that you won't ask any questions of anyone for a certain period of time, say for two months. This will force you to invent other ways that encourage clients to talk.

In the process, you will also discover that you never need to ask a question. This statement is based on my own experience. For two years, I played a game of never asking a question, and I managed to make it through life just fine. You don't even have to ask questions in an urgent situation, for example when you're trying to find the bathroom in a large department store. Instead of asking, "Where's the bathroom?" just look at any clerk and say, "Please tell me the way to the bathroom."

I'm not advocating that you give up asking questions forever. However, I am saying that the practice of refraining from asking questions temporarily can open you to other ways of speaking powerfully. And, eliminating questions almost always improves our listening.

Substitute statements for questions

One alternative to asking a question is making a statement. Instead of asking, "Can you tell me more about that?", you can say, "Well, tell me more." Or, instead of asking, "How do you feel about that?", you could say, "I'd really like to know more about your feelings."

Rephrasing the question as a statement often makes the true nature of your speaking immediately clear. For example, if you can turn the question into a statement that begins, "What I really want you to do is…" then the question was probably a specific direction or request, not an invitation to explore options.

Sometimes a question really is a question. If that's true, then you can just ask the question. At other times what you communicate could be a question *and* a statement. In that case, separate them for clarity. For example, instead of saying, "Don't you think it would be a good idea to talk to her?", you could say, "I think it would be a good idea to talk to her. What do you think about this?"

Find alternatives to asking "why?"

I avoid asking clients *why* they think, feel, or act the way they do. My commitment is to empower the person I'm coaching, and a "Why?" conversation seldom looks very empowering to me.

Questions that start with the word "why" can create problems. One problem is that asking "Why?" often leads people to make up reasons for their behavior that are incomplete, inaccurate, or both: "Why did I do that? Because I'm basically a weak person.... Because my boss is a jerk.... Because my mother dropped me on my head when I was three." We are complicated human beings, and I am not sure we can ever fully understand why we do what we do. However, given enough time, most of us can invent plenty of reasons to explain our behavior and circumstances. And, we'll probably never know for sure whether any of the explanations are accurate.

Often those explanations relate to conditions that people feel they cannot control, such as their family history, their genetic inheritance, or their acquired traits. If we ask clients why they hold on to self-defeating habits, they might say, "Everyone in my family has the same problem." Or, "My parents never gave me the kind of support I needed." Or, "I can't change that, it's part of my basic personality type."

Asking "Why?" usually leads the conversation into the past. Exploring the past in a detailed way is appropriate for Freudian psychoanalysis and other kinds of therapy, but it is not the purpose of life coaching. Dwelling in the past seldom leads us to change our behavior in the present or create powerful intentions for the future.

My experience is that people can change their behavior and produce amazing results without asking "Why?" Life coaching is more likely to make a difference when we move from "why" to "what": What's next in your life? What do you want? What is your passion? What are you willing to do to create the life of your dreams? When we carefully bring these questions to our clients, we draw them from the past into present actions that will create their future and assist them in taking responsibility for their lives.

Sometimes the question "Why?" means, "What's the purpose?" or, "What benefit are you trying to achieve?" When that's the meaning of "why", then you can get to the point directly by asking, "What's the purpose of that action?" or, "What's the benefit of that option?" This is an example of how finding an alternative to asking "Why?" can result in clearer communication.

Developing creativity and intuition

Effective coaches come to a coaching session without a fixed idea of what works or which option is the "right" option for a client. What might work during a session is something that can shift from client to client and from moment to moment.

In this kind of dynamic environment, you might find it useful to develop your creativity and intuition—your spontaneous sense of what's appropriate for *this* client in *this* moment. Use the following suggestions as ways to enhance your creativity.

Assign your intuition a place

One option is to mentally associate your intuition with a physical place. That place could be a room in your house or a clearing in the woods. It could also be the back seat of your car or a folder in your file cabinet that's labeled "intuition." When you want to access your intuition, then you can literally go to that place in your house, in your car, in the woods, or in your file cabinet.

This is similar to what people do when they go to a church to pray or when they go into a retreat center to meditate. These people have a physical place they can enter, one that helps them access the word of God or their deepest wisdom.

Imagine what clients are thinking and speak to that

Years ago when I wanted to improve my skill at speaking to large groups, I began imagining what people in the audience were thinking in response to what I was saying. Then I replied to that imagined response. For instance, if I guessed that people were thinking, "Gee, that's a weird idea," I'd say, "Now, you might think this is a weird idea, so let me say a little more about it."

One result of this practice was that I suddenly became quite funny. People laughed a lot when I correctly guessed what was on their minds. I also got more creative and was able to invent more ideas on the spot while in front of a group.

You might be thinking that this won't work for you, but I've had many people tell me that they use the same technique.

I've also found this strategy to be useful in life coaching. I just imagine what clients might think and feel in response to what I say, and then I speak to that response.

I recommend this technique as a way to develop your intuition and creativity. In a way, it allows you to view the world through the client's eyes. This fresh perspective can be a source of many new ideas.

Of course, a danger of this approach is that our sense of the client's thoughts can be off-track. If so, we could end up leading clients and steering the conversation in a direction they didn't want to go. To prevent this outcome, we can check out the direction by continually asking the client for feedback.

Put yourself on the spot

I have a long history of playing a game when I'm in front of a large group of people. When someone asks me a question, I say something like, "Well, that's a great question, so let me give you five possible answers." But, when I mention five, I very seldom have even one in mind. My practice is to generate those possibilities in the moment out of my commitment to create value for the audience.

It is somewhat embarrassing to do this when I'm in a one-on-one conversation and fail to come up with five answers. But if I say, "Let me give you five answers" in front of 150 people, then my adrenaline really starts flowing.

When that happens, I like to think I'm able to access a greater source of wisdom than my everyday mind. You can call that source of wisdom the Great Spirit, God, the universal mind, cosmic consciousness, creative intelligence, or whatever your spiritual path leads you to name it. Whatever it is, that intelligence is something that can speak through each of us.

So, you might access this infinite source of creativity by purposefully putting yourself on the spot. Just affirm your commitment to your client and announce that you have several things to say in response to his comment. Do this even before you know what you're going to say. You may be pleasantly surprised by what comes out of your mouth.

Relaxation is key to this technique. When we get relaxed, we get creative.

Admit that you're stumped and feed back the problem

At some point during a life coaching session, you might feel totally stumped. After listening to a client define her problem, you might look inside yourself for possible options to lay out on the table and find yourself drawing a big, fat zero.

If this happens, one thing you can do right away is to tell the truth: "Well, I'm stumped. Wow. This is tough, and right now I don't know where to go with this or what to do next." This response gives you permission to be empty of ideas for the moment, and that can open the door to a solution. Even if no option comes to your mind, clients might benefit from just sitting with the problem for a few minutes, inquiring deeply, and doing their own creative work.

A second option is to simply give back the problem by restating it in your own words. As you do, clients often gain enough clarity to come up with a solution on their own.

My first experience with the power of this technique took place when I was teaching computer programming. Even though I had a master's degree, my students often seemed to know more about programming than I did. Sometimes they'd bring me a problem to solve that would leave me totally stumped. So the first thing I usually said was, "Let me see if I understand what you're asking." Then, I'd restate the problem. About half the time when I did this, students would solve the problem by themselves on the spot. And when they didn't, the act of feeding back the problem created enough mental space for me to think of an idea.

I recommend this strategy to you as another way to access the infinite reservoirs of creativity that lie dormant in all of us.

Creating ceremonies and rituals

Many people in our culture are ceremony impoverished, and this fact creates an opening for us as life coaches. Part of what we can bring to our clients is ritual, celebration, and ceremony.

When referring to ceremony, I don't necessarily mean formal affairs with flowers and tuxedos. Instead, you can use any means that seem appropriate for your client—nature settings, music, incense, and even altars. You could sing, chant, meditate, or do t'ai chi on a mountaintop. You could ask clients to make a list of their resentments and then burn that list or bury it. You could ask clients to create a symbol of what they desire for the future or a monument that represents what they want to leave behind when they die. These are just a few examples, and they remind us that a sense of ritual is not a matter of externals but what we create inside ourselves.

Celebrate success

One way we can use ceremonies and rituals in a coaching relationship is to celebrate each of the client's successes and even revel in them. It is important for clients to spend at least as much time on what's working in their lives as on choosing what aspects of their lives that they want to change. Coaching runs the danger of becoming imbalanced when we lose this perspective and focus on problems and planning rather than on growth and appreciation.

When I was president of College Survival, Inc., a company of 50 people, we evaluated people frequently. We had more evaluations than any company I knew about. Every three months, our employees would be evaluated—not just by their supervisor but also by their peers and by the people they supervised. We also knew that it was tough for most people to keep looking at what to improve, so we asked that the evaluations focus just as much on celebrating what each employee already did well as on what they could improve.

Instead of talking about what's working and what's not working in clients' lives, I like to talk about what's working and what could be improved. The whole topic of "what could be improved" establishes a far more positive direction than focusing on what's not working. The question "What's not working?" confines us to only the things that are broken. I prefer to speak about things that are already working and that the client wants to work even better.

Ask about what's working well

One simple ritual you can adopt for the purpose of celebration is to regularly start coaching sessions with a request: "Tell me something about your life that is really working well." Then listen fully and extend your heartfelt appreciation for what the client says. Allow yourselves to dwell on each success, and talk about the kind of ritual or ceremony that could commemorate that positive outcome in the client's life. You can keep coming back to this topic, "Now tell me something else that is working well."

Responding when clients don't follow through

Some of your clients might promise repeatedly to take a particular action, or change a certain habit, and then fail to follow through. Perhaps they agree to exercise and never do. Perhaps they agree to finish a project at work and then refuse to even start it. Or, maybe they agree to keep a daily journal and come back session after session with a notebook full of blank pages.

When faced with such lack of follow-through, you might feel angry, sad, or afraid that the coaching relationship is going nowhere. You can acknowledge all these feelings and still respond in a way that moves the client forward.

Assist, don't insist

To begin, remember that our job as coaches is to *assist*, not to *insist*.

Now, if a client walks in with a gun to her head, I'm going to insist that she put it down. But short of saving somebody's life or preventing a crime, I can think of few situations where it's appropriate for me to insist that a client take a particular action. Insisting is not life coaching.

Our role is to open up possibilities, to lay out options, and to provide freedom. When we insist on a particular action, then we abandon that role. We can empower clients far more by drawing on other options long before we start insisting.

Hold goals lightly—and as sacred commitments

We can encourage clients to balance two attitudes toward any goal. One is to hold the goal lightly, realizing that their happiness does not depend on achieving any particular goal. The other is to hold the goal as sacred, part of their commitment to create the future that they want.

Clients who don't follow through can find this balance difficult to achieve. Some of them might take a goal so lightly that they forget about it. Others may take a goal so seriously that their lack of follow-through becomes a continual source of guilt.

As coaches, we can help clients steer a middle path between these two extremes. When clients take a goal too lightly, we can assist them to give the goal some "teeth"—for example, by suggesting that they set a timeline for achieving the goal. And when clients take goals too seriously and feel guilty about their failure to follow through, we can hold out other options, such as resetting the timeline or even releasing the goal.

Stop life coaching in certain areas

There are times when I will step out of the coaching role and draw some boundaries when I don't see that a client is making any progress in a certain area.

For instance, I might say, "As your coach, I am not going to insist that you do anything. And, I just want you to know that I will not coach you anymore about this goal because you're not taking any action. If you want to get coaching from someone else in this area of your life, you can certainly do that. And I'm happy to continue to coach you about other areas of your life."

End the life coaching relationship

If one of your clients consistently breaks major agreements, you always have the option to end the coaching relationship.

If you choose this option, I recommend that you end the relationship without a threat like: "If you don't start keeping your word, then our coaching is done!" Threats run counter to the spirit of effective life coaching in the same way that insisting, giving advice, or telling people *the* answer to their problems do.

Instead of issuing threats, you can establish from the beginning of your coaching that you want clients to keep their word, and that if they don't, you may end the coaching relationship.

Using the options to stop life coaching in certain areas, or even to end the coaching relationship, can still be consistent with your full commitment to your client. Continuing to coach people who are not generating new results can do them a disservice. By stopping coaching, you send a message: "I will get out of the way so that you can make progress on your own or with someone else."

Responding when clients seem defensive

You might find clients who occasionally resist both the content of the coaching session, the process of life coaching, or both. For example, they could react defensively when you suggest an option, or they might get visibly frustrated when you refuse to offer advice.

One response to such behaviors is to label clients as "defensive." However, there is another option I like better, and that's pretending for a moment that I created the client's defensiveness. Then I can look for ways to create a different response in my client.

Release your interpretations and judgments

What I've discovered is that clients start to react defensively when I interpret their behaviors in a judgmental way. For example, a client says, "You know, the whole problem with my life is my wife. If it weren't for my wife, I would have a great life. Every time I get up in the morning, she complains, and every time I do something great she complains. My wife is just making my life miserable."

After hearing this, I could respond with an interpretation and judgment such as, "You know, it looks to me like you are just blaming your wife and playing the role of a victim." In response, the client is probably going to become defensive.

Another option is for me to turn off my judgmental voice, affirm the client, and feed back the problem as the client sees it: "Oh, man, I got it. Your wife is the problem. It must be hard to live with a woman who is always complaining." I can make this response out of my commitment to love clients unconditionally—to avoid judging people who seem judgmental, analyzing people who seem analytical, and blaming people who seem to blame others.

In addition, I can keep bringing the client back to our overriding purpose in coaching, which is to help him create the life of his dreams. I could say, "One thing we could do is talk about ways to have a wonderful life even when you live with a woman who complains so much. But, if that's not the direction you want to go, then we could explore ways to increase your wife's happiness, ways to improve your relationship with her, or even some alternatives to living with this woman." Besides being less likely to generate defensiveness, this response gives the client many more options for moving ahead than saying, "You know, you're just playing the victim here."

When I apply a label to a person, what I'm doing is crossing over the line that divides life coaching from therapy. Therapists routinely label people with interpretations that we call diagnoses. They might describe clients as chemically dependent, depressed, obsessed, and so on. This is not only the prerogative of a therapist, it's also the therapist's job. In addition, it's totally appropriate for therapists to diagnose clients as a tool for assisting the therapist to determine a treatment to help change their client's behavior.

I hold that my job as a coach is never to confront clients with my interpretation of their behaviors or any judgments based on those interpretations. When I judge somebody for being judgmental, then *I* am being judgmental. When I blame somebody for being a blamer, then I am also blaming. In the process, I'm also paving the way for clients to act in ways that I could label defensive.

Downplay your interpretations, even when you're asked for them

Some clients who come in with judgments might ask if you concur with them. For example, my client could say, "Don't you see that my wife is making me miserable?"

If I respond out of my commitment to avoid judging the client, I could say, "Well, I don't think it matters how I see it. I am trying to look at this situation through your eyes, and it's clear to me that from your point of view, you have a wife who is making you miserable."

"But, don't you think she is really making me miserable?" the client might press.

"Actually, I think we are all responsible for our actions and our emotions. I believe that you have chosen to hang around somebody you don't enjoy being with. And, I think there are lots of other options. I would like to explore them with you."

What I'm trying to demonstrate here is that when pushed by clients, I'll tell them what I think. But even then I'll avoid confronting them with my interpretations of their behavior. When I remain non-judgmental and just feed back the client's problem, then it's more likely that clients will shift their point of view and begin to explore options for solving the problem.

Assisting clients to be more self-responsible

Imagine a scale of self-responsibility. On the high end of the scale is a person who believes that she is the author of her life. This person operates as if her levels of happiness, health, love, and wealth come from her own choices. Even when she doesn't directly control her circumstances, she believes that she can choose her response to her circumstances.

On the low end of this scale is the person who believes that he is a victim. When he speaks, you hear statements such as, "I don't have any options for dealing with this problem." "Of course I feel sad— it's rained every day for the last week." "I can't help having this problem; it's just the way I am." "I can't be happy at work because my boss is a tyrant." "There's no hope for a family like mine."

Between these two extremes are many places that clients can stand. Near the middle of the scale, for example, is the client who says, "I didn't have anything to do with the fact that my wife screamed at me, but maybe I didn't have to yell back at her." Or, "My boss is making my life miserable, but I can always go look for another job."

At a given moment, clients can stand at any point on this scale. One of the deepest joys I experience in coaching is seeing clients spend more time at the higher end of the scale. To me, this is one of the most remarkable shifts a person can make. I find that the following coaching strategies help people make that transformation.

Listen fully and affirm

Throughout this book, I refer to the power of full listening and affirmation as ways that we can assist clients to discover their passion and unlock their brilliance. Listening fully and affirming clients also helps them to move from being victims to being self-responsible.

People often conclude they're victims when they haven't experienced their genius—their abilities to think creatively and solve problems skillfully. Until they experience their genius, people are more likely to end up on the victim end of the scale.

When we listen fully, we set opposite forces in motion. In the presence of our full listening, clients can speak goals that are vitally important to them and brainstorm dozens of ways to achieve them. In the process, clients experience their power to produce new outcomes and make permanent change in their lives. Once they have that experience, it's more difficult to play the role of victim.

Offer alternatives to the language of obligation

When people believe they are victims, we hear that belief reflected in their choice of words. I describe these choices as the *language of obligation*.

Several key words and phrases point to the language of obligation. These include *I have to, I should, I need to, I must, I ought to*, and *I can't*. Clients experience little freedom, little choice, and little possibility for change when using such language. Instead, they're likely to see themselves as helpless victims of the people and circumstances in their lives.

As coaches, we can encourage people to try on new language. For example, instead of saying "I have to do that," clients can say "I might do that," "I'll try to do that," or "I could do that." These sentences are examples of the language of *possibility*—a first step out of the mud of victimhood and toward the sunlight of self-responsibility.

Clients can use their words to go even higher on the scale of self-responsibility. They can use the language of *preference* ("I'd like to meet that goal"), *passion* ("I have a burning desire to meet that goal"), *planning* ("I've created a strategy for meeting that goal next year"), and *promising* ("You can absolutely count on me to meet that goal").

Remember that words such as *might* and *try* are powerful tools for self-responsibility. Some coaches characterize these words as weak or wimpy. I disagree. *Might* and *try* are huge advances beyond *I should* and *I have to*. *Might* and *try* build bridges to a sense of possibility and language that's even more self-responsible.

I believe that the way clients string words together is a habit. With clients' permission, I can gently point out when they're using language of obligation and assist them to change that habit.

Break down large goals into smaller steps

Clients can easily become the victims of a problem that remains undissected or a goal that has not been analyzed. To help clients climb out of their victimhood, we can encourage them to break down their biggest goals into smaller, more manageable tasks.

For example, if a client says she wants a new career but has no idea where to begin, you can assist her to find a way to get started. That step could be as simple as going to the library to find one book on career planning.

Assist clients to create many options

We can also assist clients to move toward self-responsibility by promoting their most creative thinking. Clients can experience first-hand the power of brainstorming a long list of options, even when some of those options seem outrageous.

One of my clients had a goal to get up five days a week at 5:45 a.m. to meditate. I asked him to think about this and give me a list of twenty ways to adopt this new habit, including seven options that he could implement immediately. As this client spoke, I simply restated each option he invented and then I asked for more.

When using this strategy with clients, I see my job as simply to listen fully and affirm the client's thinking. Sometimes I will also write down the client's list of options. However, I seldom add to those possibilities with ideas of my own. When clients generate their own solutions, they're more likely to act on those solutions. Occasionally, I will offer to teach a technique or goal-fulfillment strategy, but I do this only with the client's permission. That's as directive as I usually want to be, especially when my goal is to promote the client's self-responsibility.

Coaching two people at once

Much of the time, life coaching involves a one-to-one interaction between a client and a coach. However, you can also invite two people who are in conflict to meet with you and assist them in improving their relationship. These people can include clients and their spouses, romantic partners, relatives, friends, coworkers, employees, supervisors, and others.

The idea of coaching couples is to improve the relationship between the two people involved *and* to improve each individual's life. With this purpose in mind, I recommend that you meet with each person individually before working with both people together.

When coaching couples, I apply most of the same techniques that I use in coaching individuals. My preference in any coaching situation is to dwell on the least directive end of the coaching continuum as explained in Chapter Three. This means assisting people to speak their goals, affirming those goals, and helping them to generate options while focusing on solutions rather than problems. With couples as with individuals, I assume that following clients' passions will unlock their brilliance and lead them to the life of their dreams.

To get the most out of sessions with couples, consider the following suggestions.

Assume that the people are committed to each other

Begin with the assumption that the people you're meeting with are committed to each other and to resolving the conflict. When you act on this assumption, you're more likely to be an effective coach.

Of course, there are times that you might want to check this assumption. For example, if your client and her spouse ask for assistance in improving their relationship, you might want to start your session by making sure that they want the relationship to continue. If not, your goal as a coach could be to help them to dissolve the relationship with celebration and love.

Build rapport with the person you know least

If you have a long-standing relationship with one person (such as your client), then put more of your initial focus on supporting the other person. Thank this person for coming to the session and acknowledge how difficult it might be for them to be present with you and your client.

Define and celebrate your role in the session

To clarify your role, begin the session by making a statement such as, "I'm glad to be here with you. As I see it, my job is to assist you to speak openly to each other, and there's not much that I would rather do than be present to that kind of heartfelt communication. I also think that I can fulfill my role most effectively by giving no advice but by allowing you to do most of the talking. My role is to facilitate your communication."

Assist people to share the conversation space

After you ask the people present to define the problem, assist both of them to speak fully. People in relationship easily create conflicts when one person does either nearly all of the talking or all of the listening. Your role at this point can be to slow down the communication and ensure that both people get an adequate chance to speak.

Assist people to separate speaking and listening

Allow people to speak in turn and to speak until they've said everything they want to say. If someone interrupts the person who's speaking, you can gently intervene: "I realize that you may not agree, and remember that you will have a chance to reply in a few minutes. For the moment, I ask that you just listen."

One way to assist with separating speaking and listening is to have a symbol or a token that the couple passes back and forth between each other. I have a crystal that is about the size of a pencil that I call a "truth stick." I give it to one person in the couple and explain that when she is holding it, her job is to tell the truth, the whole truth and nothing but the truth. I explain to the other that his job is to just listen. Once the person with the truth stick is done communicating, she passes the stick to the other whose job now becomes telling the truth. This symbol acts as a physical reminder that effective communication is enhanced when we either send or receive instead of trying to do both at the same time.

Also ask people to talk to each other, not to you.

Assist people to separate and summarize key messages

People who feel upset often have a lot to say—not just one or two points but maybe eight, nine, ten, or more. You can create tremendous value by stopping the speaker after each one of those points has been made. Then ask the person listening to summarize that point to the speaker's satisfaction.

Make everyone "right"

People in conflict frequently come to the table with the assumption that only one of them has the most reasonable point of view. In their opinion, one person is "right" and the other is "wrong."

As a coach, you can hold out another option—that each person's viewpoint has potential value and that each person deserves to be heard. Listen fully to both people and affirm the goals that each speaks. Whenever possible, assist them to combine their goals so that they both get what they want in life. I describe this as moving from *or* to *and*.

For example, when working with a married couple, you might find that the man wants to move to a new city while the woman wants to maintain relationships with friends where the couple currently lives. This couple might assume that they can either move or continue key relationships. As their coach, you can help them generate dozens of options for moving *and* maintaining their friendships.

Ask clients to share the things they've withheld

Before people talk about a particular problem or goal, ask them to make a list of undelivered communication and then read it out loud. This list can include the hopes, dreams, secrets, upsets, and embarrassments they've never revealed to the other person. Encourage clients to consider every area of their lives—work, sex, money, kids, spirituality, and more.

Many couples are terrified to do this at first. Sharing what they've withheld can lead to discomfort and put the relationship at risk. However, my experience is that secrets block intimacy between people. When those secrets are delivered, the relationship is far more likely to bloom than to dissolve. Your presence as a facilitator to this kind of communication creates an environment of safety.

Of course, there is a possibility that such an exercise will put so much stress on the relationship that it will end. Communication is risky. As always, when working with clients, make sure that what you suggest is seen as one possible option.

Use the empty chair technique

In addition to meeting with two or more people, you can assist individual clients to do a role-play that promotes full communication. Ask them to imagine that a person they've not communicated fully with is sitting in the same room. Set up an empty chair for this imagined person to "sit" in. Then ask clients to speak to that person as if the person were actually present. You can sometimes ask clients to shift chairs and speak as if they were the other person.

For instance, if the client is in conflict with her husband, ask her to imagine that he is sitting in the empty chair and then request that she tell her husband everything that she's been withholding from him.

The empty chair technique has other powerful uses. One variation is to ask clients to imagine that the brilliant person within them is sitting in the empty chair. Clients can then communicate with that part of themselves. You can also put a key figure from the client's past or a person that the client greatly admires in that chair. For example, the coach can ask the client to list three people whom she admires and then ask her to imagine speaking to one of those three people. The client picks the person, sits in a chair, assumes the persona of that person, and talks about who she is. She then shifts the chair back so as to be herself again and then describes to the person in the empty chair the life dilemma. The client then shifts back to assume the persona of the person she respects and talks back.

Coaching clients when you don't know or don't have it handled

As a life coach, I can really feel stumped and lose confidence quickly when venturing into specific areas of a client's life. I see this happening in two types of situations. One situation when I lose confidence is when I'm about to enter an area that I know something about but don't have "handled" in my personal life. For example, a client wants coaching about overcoming procrastination. I know some strategies for solving this problem, but I might be a person who procrastinates all the time. Immediately I wonder how I can ever coach this person.

The other situation when I might feel stumped is when the client brings up a topic I know nothing about. Perhaps my client is the chief financial officer for a large corporation and wants coaching about his career options. Or, maybe my client is a neurosurgeon who wants to increase his professional effectiveness. I could feel ineffective as I face the fact that I know little about large corporate finances and nothing about neurosurgery.

Fortunately, we as coaches can be effective in working with any area of a client's life—even if we don't have the area handled ourselves, and even if we know nothing about it. Before referring clients to a consultant who does know their specialty, experiment with the following options.

Admit that you don't know

You can begin by practicing something that you ask clients to do—speak candidly. When you don't have a problem handled or know anything about a topic, you can simply tell the truth. It may be harder to tell the truth to yourself about your limitations than to tell your clients. At the same time, this admission allows the coaching to proceed on an authentic basis and creates a foundation for the options that follow.

Focus on process

As a life coach, you are someone skilled in processes. Even if you haven't solved a particular problem in your own life, you do know strategies for solving any problem. Even when you've not changed the habit of procrastination, you still know strategies for changing any habit. And even if you don't know about the kind of communication that takes place between neurosurgeons in an operating room, you do know strategies for speaking powerfully and listening effectively in any situation.

Your skill in articulating general processes creates value for clients far beyond your knowledge of any particular subject area. The particular processes that I recommend you focus on are summarized at the end of Chapter Five and detailed in my book *Falling Awake*.

Distinguish coaching from consulting

When coaching clients in their area of expertise, also keep in mind the distinction between being a coach and being a consultant.

A consultant is someone who's reached a level of mastery in a specific subject. If I'm going to consult people about neurosurgery, for instance, then I'd better know a lot about neurosurgery. I could even spend a major portion of my time teaching other neurosurgeons about ways to do specific parts of their job.

But as a coach, my role is different: I am not a consultant, and I'm not there to teach clients. As a coach, I say to people, "Discover what works for you, and trust your brilliance."

Remember the benefits of ignorance

When assisting a client, you could be even more effective than someone who knows the client's area of specialty. In this case, your ignorance is your strength. You can bring a fresh, outside perspective to the conversation and see issues and options that a specialist might overlook. Also, you don't have any preconceived notions about how to solve the client's particular problem. But, you do have a bundle of powerful strategies for solving *any* problem.

What's more, you know that the client is brilliant. You know that when given a skilled listener and the chance to generate a long list of possible solutions, the client will create powerful and effective options.

Learn about the subject

When you don't have it handled or you don't know about it, you always have the option to learn more about it. Of course, you may never become a neurosurgeon. But, you can learn some of the key terms of this specialty so that you use more of the client's language.

For two years, I coached an NBA coach. He referred to me as the "head coach's head coach." The problem was that I knew nothing about basketball: I'd never played it, I'd never watched it. When I first started working with this man, I wanted to know something about his career so I called my son-in-law whose profession and avocation is sports. He gave me enough of a tutorial that I could at least follow my client's stories.

Bringing your specialty carefully

Besides knowing the process of coaching, many of us bring training, experience, and education in other specific areas. For example, I have a background in accounting, computer programming, and starting and running a business. When working with clients who have questions about these topics, I could draw on this background. You could do the same when coaching clients in your specialty area.

Although I think it's great to get in touch with our areas of specialty, I recommend that we generally avoid bringing them into the life coaching experience. The danger is that we could over-apply our specialties. Our expertise can become a hammer, and everything the client says can start to look like a nail. To a coach who's also a chemical dependency counselor, every client could look like an addict. To a coach who is a financial counselor, every problem could look like a problem with money.

For this reason, I recommend that coaches avoid promoting their areas of specialty while marketing. If you say that you are a life coach who specializes in health and vitality because you know a lot about exercise and nutrition, then you could quickly run into problems. One of your clients might come into a session thinking, "My real problem is that I'm not getting along with my wife, but I don't know if I should bring that up; it doesn't have any thing to do with health or vitality." Even if you tell clients that you'll work with them about anything, that message can easily get lost in the promotion of your specialty in health and nutrition.

Our clients experience the power and possibility of life coaching when we're willing to look at every area of their lives and embrace any problem that they experience. We can serve people most effectively when we lift our eyes to a broader horizon and be cautious about promoting our own specialties.

Acknowledging mistakes that life coaches make

Life coaches can make a variety of mistakes. From my point of view, some of the major mistakes are the following.

Deciding what's best for our clients and then steering them

Rather than just offering possibilities, we sometimes try to lead the show: "My client works a lot of overtime, so I better do something to help him take more time off.... My client talks a lot about the past, so she should talk more about what she wants in the future.... My client is overweight, so the next thing for us to do is focus on exercise and nutrition."

In my point of view, all of that direction is a mistake. It's not our job as life coaches to steer clients in any direction except the direction that they choose. Of course, there are situations when I will get directive. If my client is depressed and wants to end his life, I am going to be very directive and steer the client toward a therapist or a suicide hotline.

Judging clients instead of affirming them

"You're pretty slippery about keeping your agreements…. The way you spoke was not self-responsible…. You're just not being candid here." These are all examples of my judgments, which, even if accurate, have no place in a coaching relationship.

Making mistakes and hiding them

When I screw up and then cover it up, clients can go away confused. They probably know that I goofed, and they wonder why I didn't admit it. Or, they start questioning their own intuition and ability to notice mistakes.

Telling a client's secret

I believe that confidentiality is broken not only when we tell someone's secret but also when we reveal that someone *has* a secret. "I've been coaching John, and something really big is coming up in his life, but I can't tell you what it is," is a breach of confidence.

Spending too little time with clients

In a sense, life coaching is a little like giving penicillin. Penicillin's a wonderful drug unless we give too little of it. Then the bacteria we're trying to kill become resistant. Something analogous to this happens when we enroll coaching clients, set up an expectation that their lives will improve dramatically, and then schedule only two hours with them a month for three months. No life coach is going to live up to that expectation, no matter how good she is. Assisting people to alter the quality of their lives takes time.

When starting with a new coaching client, I ask for a commitment from them of at least four hours per month for at least 12 months.

Thinking that we know what the mistakes are

Perhaps the biggest mistake life coaches can make does not appear in the above list. That mistake is thinking that we know that any particular coaching behavior is a mistake. Any coaching behavior can be effective at one point, and it can be a mistake at another point.

Some of the things listed—when done in an appropriate way at an appropriate time—will be useful and even empower the client. When we start making absolute rules about what's right or what's wrong in coaching, then we diminish our options. We approach clients with formulas instead of an overriding commitment to doing whatever moves them forward.

Acknowledging mistakes allows us to learn from and even celebrate them. We can often learn far more from our mistakes than from our successes. That kind of learning becomes possible when we candidly admit our mistakes and shine a light on them long enough to let them teach us.

Chapter Five
Possible Topics to Teach

In life coaching relationships, there are times when it makes sense for us to assume the role of teacher. Following are examples of skills and distinctions that life coaches can teach to clients to assist them in creating a more wonderful life. In addition to the list in this chapter, there are dozens of other related ideas presented in my books *Falling Awake* and *Creating Your Future: Five Steps to the Life of Your Dreams* and in the book I co-authored with Stan Lankowitz entitled *Human Being: A Manual for Happiness, Health, Love, and Wealth*. In all life coaching interactions, I think it is important that we have our clients' permission and verify their interest in learning these skills before we teach them. During a coaching session, I want to let my client lead. If I have something to teach, I will start by offering this option to her and I will not proceed until I am clear that teaching is what my client wants.

Get the most from life coaching

One way you can serve clients is to teach them a whole smorgasbord of ways for them to get the most of the life coaching relationship. Once you have taught these ways of being an effective client, you can revisit the list on a regular basis.

By presenting ways to create value from coaching, you assist clients to create the life of their dreams more quickly. Following are suggestions for clients about getting the most from life coaching.

Clear your slate

To create value from life coaching, make space for it in your life. Set aside other projects for the time being when it's time for your scheduled session. Handle potential interruptions before the coaching session—telephone calls, bathroom breaks, dinner plans. If you get distracted during a session, report that fact so your coach can help you choose what to do about it. If it makes sense, reschedule the coaching for another time.

Raise the stakes

Set high expectations for the coaching and for yourself. Pretend that you're paying $500 an hour for this service. Then brainstorm a list of things you would do to ensure that you get this much value. Review your list for ideas you can use at the coaching session that you are about to begin.

Communicate fully

Coaching is more likely to work when you are brave, candid, and outspoken. Be willing to tell your coach everything; nothing is too small or too large. Your coach might come to know more about you than almost anyone else, and that's usually a desirable outcome.

It pays to be candid when you experience difficulties with the coaching process—or with your coach. If you feel upset about anything that happens during a session, report the fact immediately. This assists your coach to help you move past the upset.

Own the coaching

Life coaching assists you to create your own ideas for solving problems and invent your own strategies for reaching your goals. To promote this kind of creativity, avoid statements such as: "My coach says I should do this," or, "I'm doing this because my coach told me to." Those kinds of comments might be accurate when applied to a teacher or consultant; they're not a great reference to a life coach.

One of the main uses of coaching is to trigger your enthusiasm and unleash your personal brilliance. This is more likely to happen when you take responsibility for your choices.

Summarize discoveries and intentions

Keep a record of the discoveries and intentions you create while meeting with a life coach. Take notes during the meeting, then review, edit, summarize, and expand them afterwards. Post these notes in a place where you'll see them often, such as a bathroom mirror or car dashboard.

Consider sending your notes to your life coach. The power of this strategy is that your coach gets to see what you're learning. This learning can be amplified and developed in future sessions.

Effective life coaching reinforces the cycle of discovery, intention, and action. Say that while meeting with your coach, you gain a new insight about yourself—that you want to work only part-time. That's an example of discovery. To get the most value from that discovery, turn it into a clear intention, such as a goal to cut back to 30 hours of work per week, and to accomplish that within six months. Then turn your intention into action: start working less this week.

Following through on your intentions will probably reveal new insights that, again, you can translate into intentions and action. Each time you move through this cycle of discovery-intention-action, you create new value and new outcomes in your life.

Speak your dreams

In daily life, people often forget to lift their eyes to the horizon, to the most long-term, comprehensive vision of what they want. They get lost in the details of their daily schedules and to-do lists. They see the trees, not the forest—the most urgent tasks instead of the most valuable ones.

By meeting with a life coach, you prevent this outcome. Use your coach as your dream-catcher and goal magnet. Speak your short-term and long-term goals. Speak your life purpose, your dreams, and your passions. Consider asking your coach to help you create a life plan—a detailed, long-term vision of what you want to have, do, and be for the rest of your life. Ask your coach to write down your dreams, hold them in her consciousness, and keep bringing you back to them. Then fulfill those dreams by taking action.

Many of us work and live in places where no one asks us what we want for the short-term and long-term future. And even when we start to say what we want, there's often nobody to listen. What a gift it is to meet with a coach whose job description is to hold our dreams as sacred creations!

Creating the future

By creating the future, I mean assisting clients to speak in detail about what they want over the long term and how they intend to get it. This activity includes creating goals and action plans for every area of their lives.

The following ideas are a condensation of the strategies that I present in the second chapter of my book, *Falling Awake*, and throughout *Creating Your Future*.

I consistently ask my clients about what they want in their lives. I invite them to consider what they would do if they won the lottery and could suddenly afford to do anything they choose. If a client says that he wants to retire in three years and live in the Caribbean, I know that this goal is entirely possible, but that it won't happen on its own. With my client, we quickly create many paths to reach that goal. Then we create even more outlandish visions, dreams, and plans.

I also ask people to create their long-range future—what they want to see happen in 20 years, 50 years, even 100 years. I invite them to look decades into the future and to launch projects that extend well beyond their lifetimes. Then I ask what clients would like to do in the short-term about their long-range vision. People quickly discover that creating the long-range future makes a difference in what they choose to do this year, this month, and this week.

You can assist clients to get past any obstacles they encounter to creating their future. Below are two obstacles that may come up for your clients along with possible solutions. Following these are several strategies clients can use to experience the power of creating the future.

Reconcile goal setting and spontaneity

Your clients might quickly voice a typical objection to creating the future: "If I set goals, I'll become uptight. I'll sacrifice my freedom. I won't be able to go with the flow or be spontaneous." When you hear this objection, you can respond with the following ideas.

REPLACE *OR* WITH *AND*

People often approach this topic with an "either-or" mind-set: "I can *either* set goals *or* be spontaneous." Suggest that clients rephrase that statement, replacing the *or* with *and*: "I can set goals *and* be spontaneous." This small step can put clients' thinking on a new track and open possibilities.

In presenting this option to clients, I sometimes present an analogy. For me, setting goals is like setting off for a day of white-water rafting and choosing where I'll take a break to eat lunch. I want a spot that's sandy and flat with lots of sun, and pleasant smells. With that thought in mind, I put my boat in the water and start paddling. Naturally, I'm going to go with the flow; when you're white-water rafting, that's about all you can do. But the power of having a goal is that I'm more likely to notice the flat, sunny places. And whenever I spot such a place, I can see if I can get the boat to that place so I can eat. Paradoxically, I'm going with the flow *and* achieving my goal.

This analogy makes another point: setting and achieving goals do not have to be cumbersome and difficult processes. Rather, clients can just fix a goal in mind and make moment-to-moment choices that move them closer toward it.

EXPERIMENT WITH THE IDEA

If you try to argue for the benefits of goal setting, you could generate resistance on the client's part. Instead, you can meet clients halfway by acknowledging their objections and inviting them to just give the process a try. For instance, you could say, "When you create goals, you might lose spontaneity—and you might not. Each person will probably have a different experience. You could just experiment with goal setting for a short time and see whether it offers any benefits for you."

EXPLORE SEVERAL PATHS TO ACHIEVING THE GOAL

With your help, clients can invent many different pathways to achieving a single goal. For example, a person who wants to make more friends could achieve that goal by joining a church, taking a community education class, starting a book club, or taking countless other actions.

Just as clients can select from several different routes when driving to work, they can also choose from several routes to achieving a goal. Seeing this fact is often enough to help clients reconcile spontaneity and goal setting.

REVISE GOALS AT ANY TIME

It is valuable to remember that once we write an idea down it does not mean it is set in stone. Any goal, dream, or desire can be rewritten and revised, or even abandoned, at any time.

Suppose your client sets a goal to retire at age 50. On her 49th birthday, she reviews her retirement funds and discovers that she has only enough money saved to support herself for a few years without working. This fact is no reason to abandon the goal. Instead, she can reset the timeline and create a new a financial plan for retiring at age 55.

Clients might ask, "If you keep resetting the goal, then is there any value in having the goal in the first place?" My answer is an emphatic "Yes!" Setting a goal often leads to immediate and beneficial changes in our day-to-day actions. And even when an initial goal proves to be unworkable, we can scale it back, set a new timeline, or modify the goal in some other way so that it becomes achievable.

CALL IT SOMETHING ELSE
Some clients will warm up to the process of setting and achieving goals when you use different words to describe it. This is one reason that I talk about *creating the future* instead of *planning*. Other clients might respond favorably if you refer to the process as *designing your life, choreographing your dream,* or *clarifying your vision*.

DON'T SET GOALS
When clients are still not convinced by the suggestions listed above and fear that goal setting will inhibit them, remember that no one *has* to set goals. Life coaching can include problem-solving, conflict resolution, emotional release, and dozens of other activities besides planning. Our path is to let clients choose the direction of the coaching and trust their wisdom.

Reconcile goal setting with God's will

Another obstacle to creating the future sometimes occurs with clients who have certain religious beliefs. These clients find it hard to reconcile the idea of creating the future with following God's will.

My 20 years of experience in teaching college students about self-responsibility has given me plenty of practice with this obstacle. In some Christian schools, the whole concept that we create our life experiences does not go over well. Even so, I've discovered two ideas that often assist these people to embrace the process of creating their future.

The first is that creating your future involves listening to God. Some ways to generate goals include joining a religious community, praying, and asking to receive a knowledge of God's will. Then we can set goals that align with God's will.

Second, our job is to help God create what God wants. Once we have goals that reflect God's will, we can choose ways to achieve those goals. For this purpose, God granted us some manner of free will. According to this line of reasoning, God reveals *what* to do in general—to love people, keep the Ten Commandments, and so on—and lets us choose specific *ways* to do those things and whether or not to even do them.

I love the line in the movie *Oh, God* where God (played by George Burns) appears to a store clerk (played by John Denver). There's a scene where God says, "You know, I just told you *what* to do. You've got to figure out the *how* on your own." That's a wonderful message for the person who wonders if creating the future is aligned with God's will.

Assist clients to balance their conversation space

When I begin working with people, I often notice that their conversation is dominated by the past. They talk primarily about events that took place yesterday, last month, last year, or even last decade.

We have a second option, which is to focus more of our conversation on the present. When we do, we can celebrate the joys of the moment. The present moment is the point in time when we fully experience creativity, great food, passionate sex, and pure fun. As children, we naturally focused much of our consciousness on the present moment. When people learn meditation and other spiritual practices, they start regaining that childhood ability.

We also have a third option, one that's fairly uncommon: creating the future. This option involves speaking in detail about what we want for the future and how we plan to get it. When I listen to people, I seldom hear them creating the future. Instead, I hear them worrying about the future or predicting it. By the way, prediction is even where most futurists reside—predicting future events by extrapolating from current trends. I am suggesting creating the future instead of worrying about it or predicting it.

By offering these options, we can assist our clients to balance their speaking, reading, writing, and thinking—their total conversation space. They can devote about one-third of this space to the past, another third to the present, and a final third to the future. And when speaking about the future, they can shift from worrying and predicting what they think *will* happen to choosing what they *want* to happen. When clients make this shift, they start speaking their passions, dreams, purposes, goals, and plans.

We offer our clients a valuable service by mirroring their language. With their permission, we can point out when clients are talking primarily about the past, the present, or the future. We can also request that they experiment with creating the future.

Highlight specific goals

Clients can begin creating the future by speaking general goals: "I want to be happier." "I'd like to be healthier." "I want to have a job that I love." "I want fulfilling relationships."

General, long-term goals such as these are wonderful. And, it is even more effective when clients translate these goals into specific, short-term goals that they can start accomplishing right away. By *specific*, I mean goals that point to measurable, detailed, and observable results to be accomplished by specific dates. There's great power in this level of specificity. When clients create a specific goal, they're more likely to meet it—and to know when they've missed it. When I listen to clients, I often highlight any specific goals they speak and suggest that they create more.

Focus on what *and stay flexible about* how

As I review recent history, I see that few large-scale and worthwhile goals were ever taken on by people who knew exactly how they were going to meet those goals. Recently, I watched Martin Luther King's "I have a dream" speech on video, and I realized something for the first time: when King said he had a dream, he didn't also say, "I have a plan." His entire speech was about *what* he wanted to see in the future, not about *how* to accomplish it. The clarity and power of his vision was enough to fuel a civil rights movement, even before specific plans for the movement were in place.

If you review your own life, you can discover a similar process at work. When you began large projects, you were probably clear about *what* results you wanted. However, you probably didn't know exactly *how* you were going to achieve those results. Chances are that you figured out *how* along the way. And, if you had a detailed plan at the beginning of the project, you probably changed or even abandoned that plan in favor of another. Even so, your vision and dream was enough to pull you forward into the future.

I am not saying that we should ignore the question of *how* to accomplish a goal. What I mean is that *how* needs to be continually re-invented in the moment as we take action toward *what* we want. Otherwise, we can get so caught up in *how* that our vision of *what* becomes blurred. When the *how* is something we invented in the past, then we're often out of touch with the realities of the present, and our actions can produce inferior results. Our moment-to-moment actions can be dictated by a rich, compelling, and detailed vision of the future—not by a possibly outdated plan invented in the past.

Use two-week planning

In order to avoid a life that is overscheduled, I have developed a useful technique and taught it to hundreds of people. This technique involves planning every two weeks.

What I recommend is just a straightforward process for planning two weeks in advance. Though the process is relatively simple, most people won't do it without some guidance. By taking the time to teach this technique and then guide clients through the following steps, you provide them with a valuable and unique service.

1. LIST UPCOMING TASKS
Ask clients to describe each significant task they want to complete in the next 14 days. You can list each task on a separate 3×5 card or in a computer. Putting these tasks in a computer or on individual 3×5 cards allows them to be easily sorted and prioritized.

To get a realistic picture of what's actually on a client's plate, keep prompting her to describe what she *needs* to do—the urgent tasks in her life—and what she *wants* to do for personal development and fun.

When I've done this step with clients, we typically end up with dozens of cards. And these tasks run the gamut from *buy new shoes before the sales meeting* or *spend more time with my daughter* to *paint the deck* or *hire a new secretary*.

2. ESTIMATE THE TIME NEEDED FOR EACH TASK AND ARRIVE AT A TOTAL
When clients come face-to-face with their detailed list of tasks, they often get the impression that it looks completely undoable. That happens for a reason: it *is* undoable. There are just too many tasks allotted for too little time.

To deal with this problem, go back to each task you listed and ask your client to estimate the number of hours needed to complete it. To make this step most useful, keep quizzing her for a realistic estimate and be liberal. Clients often discover that it takes about twice as long to complete a task as they initially suspect, especially when they have little experience at monitoring their time. For example, if a client needs to hire a new secretary and estimates that this will take four hours, you might ask if eight hours would be more accurate.

After you and your client finish assigning a time to each task, add up the times to get a total number of hours.

3. ASK YOUR CLIENT HOW MANY HOURS SHE WANTS TO WORK

Next, divide the tasks into two categories, work and non-work. Then ask your client how many hours she wants to work in the next two weeks.

When you make this request, she might say, "I'll just work until I get it all done." I suggest that you not accept that answer. Instead, ask her how many hours she'd ideally like to work each week for the next two weeks. To make this process even more concrete, subdivide that total into daily work hours. Ask her how many hours she wants to work next Monday, next Tuesday, next Wednesday, and so on.

4. PRIORITIZE TASKS

Now comes the fun part—you and your client get to prioritize.

To begin, ask your client which tasks she wants to do during the next two weeks and which ones she's willing to carry forward to a later two-week period. Also ask which tasks could be delegated to other people.

Then go through the remaining tasks with your client and assign each one a level of priority. I often use the *ABC priority system*:

- An *A priority* means that clients are absolutely committed to completing the task during the next two weeks ("I've promised to get this done").

- A *B priority* means that clients would like to complete the task within the next two weeks but are not absolutely committed to getting it done ("It would be nice to get this done, but it's okay if I don't").

- A *C priority* means that clients just see the task as a useful possibility ("This is just a possibility, and I'll do it only if everything else gets done").

Sometimes I use another way to describe these levels: *A-priority* tasks are *promises*, *B-priority* tasks are *plans*, and *C-priority* tasks are *possibilities*.

5. TOTAL AND ADJUST THE NUMBER OF HOURS FOR HIGH-PRIORITY TASKS
At this point, I ask my client to add up the number of hours she will need to complete her A-priority tasks, both at work and at home. And generally what happens is that the client makes another sobering discovery: she is over-committed. For example, she has 130 hours worth of tasks to complete at work during the next two weeks, but she only wants to work 100 hours during that period.

Now my client gets to choose ways to decrease the hours needed for her A-priority tasks. "Well, I'll just work faster," she might say. This strategy doesn't account for interruptions, last-minute crises, and other surprises. More viable options include:

- Downgrading some *A-priority* tasks to the level of *B*'s or *C*'s.
- Delegating some *A*'s.
- Moving some *A*'s to a later two-week period.
- Eliminating some *A*'s altogether.

Keep experimenting until the total number of hours for *A-priority* work tasks is actually *less* than the total number of hours that your client would like to work during the next two weeks. So, for instance, if she wants to work 100 hours, keep whittling away at those *A*'s until they total 80 or 90. You can do the same for non-work tasks.

6. SCHEDULE HIGH-PRIORITY TASKS
Finally, ask your client to take her calendar and block out an appropriate number of hours for *key A-priority* tasks. (It's not necessary or even useful to schedule all the *A*'s.)

Many clients find that entering these tasks in a calendar is a useful step. They find, like I do, that scheduling a specific date and time for a task means that it's more likely to be completed.

To help your client create the most value from this step, suggest that she schedule times for non-work activities as well as work-related tasks. This is a powerful way to make time for important tasks that can easily get shoved aside, such as exercise, reading, getting together with friends, going to movies, and other recreational activities.

When clients start bringing their daily activities in line with what they truly want and find ways to balance work with play, they can uncover a new source of energy and fulfillment.

Discover strengths and special interests

Some clients may ask you for help in discovering their strengths and special areas of interest so they can create their future consistent with their abilities. You can assist them to gain this self-knowledge and act on it while they also maintain a balance in their lives.

FOLLOW PASSION
To help your client get in touch with his specialty, ask him to go where his passion goes. Invite him to look first at what he loves to do. I think most people can trust their passion. If they love doing something, then they've probably found their specialty.

SURVEY FRIENDS
Another powerful strategy that people seldom use is to conduct an informal survey. Suggest that your client pose this question to his

friends and relatives: "What do you think I'm good at?" He may be surprised and pleased at what these people report.

I've done such surveys several times and have been shocked at what people say my specialties are. Typically these are skills that I take for granted, such as the ability to handle details and maintain focused attention. Often my first reaction is, "Doesn't everybody do this well?" Of course they don't, and making this discovery has expanded my perception of my own strengths.

ASK CLIENTS WHAT THEY *WISH* FOR AS A SPECIALITY

When clients remain unclear about their chosen specialty, you can ask them what they *wish* their specialty could be. My guess is that when people answer this question, about half the time they will end up telling you what they already excel at doing.

For example, if you ask me what I wish to specialize in, I would answer that I want to specialize in speaking candidly, authentically, and courageously to people. I also know that when I look closely, I see that this really *is* my specialty; I just want to get better at it. When I review my strengths, what I see is how far I have to go and how much I have yet to learn in this area. But when I reflect on how few people demonstrate this skill, I can see that I've already developed it to a high degree.

Posing this simple question, "What do you wish your specialty was?" is another under-rated tool that clients can use to more accurately assess their skills and strengths.

REMEMBER THAT SPECIALTIES CAN BE OVER-APPLIED

While empowering us to move into effective action, our specialties can also limit us. Strengths we take to an extreme become liabilities. When we become over-reliant on a particular talent, then we're probably not developing others.

After the company I founded had been in business for about five years, people criticized some of us on the staff—particularly me—

for "making candor king." Now, speaking candidly has been one of my primary values for years. And while I still think that candor is wonderful, I know that when taken to an extreme it can insult people or even hurt them.

For me this has been a powerful example of how a specialty can be over-applied. I see now that there is something more important than candor, and that is love. If love isn't in place in a relationship, then candid speaking may not work. Often it's useful for people to put love first and then cultivate candor.

In addition to helping clients get in touch with their specialty, a coach can uncover any costs of over-relying on their specialty. The coach can assist clients to invent ways for keeping those strengths in check.

Solving problems

Focus on solutions rather than problems

We can assist clients to shift from a focus on problems to a focus on solutions. Most people spend the bulk of their time and their mental energy dwelling on their problems and only a small portion creating solutions. As a life coach, we can reverse that balance so that clients spend the bulk of their time focused on solutions. This will amount to a huge shift in their conversation that can rapidly generate new actions and guide the client to their genius.

As a bridge to discovering solutions, you can promote brainstorming—creating many possible solutions to a given problem. This kind of creativity flourishes when people refrain from evaluating ideas at first. Ask your client to verbalize even her most "ridiculous" ideas and then you can affirm them. That leaves the door open for ways to turn ridiculous ideas into doable action plans: "You want to start your life over again by leaving town? Well, you might be able to get many of the same benefits by taking a sabbatical and traveling…. You want to stop drinking and keep experiencing pleasure every day? Great. You could find dozens of healthful ways to get high, including exercising." This technique can be even more powerful when clients generate doable options from wild and crazy ideas.

Consider two models for problem-solving

Once your clients perceive the benefits of focusing on solutions, you can teach some general strategies for problem-solving.

There are many models that describe the process of moving from problems to solutions. One model that you can recommend to clients involves the following six steps (five of which are about solutions):

1. *Clearly state the problem.* This step alone might be enough to reveal a workable solution.
2. *Brainstorm a long list of possible solutions.* Allow even the wildest and craziest options.
3. *Sleep on that list of solutions.* Allow some time to pass before you evaluate them. This permits even more possible solutions to bubble up into conscious awareness. Prayer, affirmations, and creative visualization can yield additional options.
4. *Analyze the benefits and costs* of each possible solution.
5. *Choose and implement a solution* without regarding it as the only "right" solution.
6. *Review the results of implementing the solution.*

Then repeat the above steps as many times as you want, working with a new solution or new definition of the problem.

You might also find value in a second model of problem-solving. This process has only four steps:

1. *Clearly state the problem.*
2. *Create a long list of the costs of having this problem.*
3. *Also create a long list of possible benefits that flow from having the problem.* Though some clients might resist the notion that they benefit from problems, I recommend that you encourage them to keep looking.

This step is especially useful when clients are working with long-standing problems. When the benefits of a problem outweigh the costs, then the problem can stay in place for months or even years.

For example, one of the persistent problems in my life is that I over-schedule and take on too many commitments. However, this problem creates significant benefits for me. For one, I feel more important and useful when I'm busy. Also, when I'm extremely busy, I find it easier to say no to requests and projects that don't interest me.

4. *Create ways to maintain the benefits without the costs.* In my own case, I could take on fewer projects with greater potential impact. That way I could maintain the benefits (making a valuable contribution to the world) while decreasing the costs (over-commitment). I can also develop a new habit of saying no when I don't want to do something even when I am not too busy.

Changing habits

The power of changing habits becomes clear to clients when they try on a new idea—that most of the things they want to change about themselves are habits. For example, I think maybe even happiness is a habit. I think that complaining is a habit. I think that lack of energy might also be a habit. I also think that much depression is a habit—not clinical depression, but the kind of depression that occurs with people who occasionally say, "I'm feeling sad and depressed." Our level of self-esteem, our ways of solving problems, and even many aspects of our appearance (like how we hold our face) are also habits. I see our behaviors and personalities as mostly a collection of habits.

This is not the way that most people view the world. When clients reveal their sadness, lack of energy, low self-esteem, or other problems, they often attribute these problems to factors beyond their control: their genetic predisposition, their personality type, or their cultural background. I recently spoke with someone who said, "I grew up in New York City, and New Yorkers are pretty aggressive, so don't try to change me."

Seeing our problems as habits instantly grants us power, and for a simple reason: habits can be changed. If depression, lack of energy, and low self-esteem are the result of genetics, personality, or culture, then there's probably not much we can do about them. But if these problems and many others are simply habits, then there is much we can do about them. Changing these parts of our lives can be as simple as changing a habit.

During a coaching session, one of my clients said, "I know I'm harsh with my coworkers and easily get angry with them. I guess I should probably figure out the reasons that I act this way. I've been in therapy about this and tried to get to the root of this behavior. But I still find myself yelling at people. Why am I so harsh?"

"I'd like to offer you another option," I replied. "Instead of trying to figure out why you act so harshly, you could assume that harshness is just a habit. And, if you're willing to experiment with this point of view, then you might be able to change this habit in short order. If you like, I could share with you a simple procedure for changing habits that's worked wonders for me and many of my clients."

He agreed to this option and put the procedure to work in his life. At a later session, he reported the results: "I haven't yelled at anyone for three weeks. And, my coworkers say that they see a huge change in my attitude and behavior."

Your clients could achieve similar results by experimenting with the following 4-step method for changing a habit.

1. Commit to change

Changing habits begins with commitment. This step is the foundation for the others. Clients can make huge strides to changing habits simply out of their ironclad commitment to alter their behavior. And, clients can commit to change even before they know exactly how they're going to change the habit.

People often ask me how long it takes to change a habit. I answer, "Somewhere between five minutes and 21 years. It depends on the habit." I changed a lifelong habit of chewing my fingernails in three hours. I'm still working on my changing the habit of getting upset when people around me are upset.

Acquiring other habits, such as exercising regularly or using two-week plans, can take a few weeks. Instead of getting locked into a conversation about how long the habit change will take, I encourage clients to keep an open mind and move on to the next step.

2. Set up a feedback system

After committing to change, I ask clients to set up a feedback system so that they can monitor their behavior. There are many types of feedback systems ranging from simple to sophisticated, such as:

- Marking your calendar each time you perform the new behavior.
- Making a chart. For example, if you want to adopt the habit of regular exercise, you could create a chart that displays each day of the week and mark the chart each day that you exercise.
- Asking friends or relatives to tell you when they see you reverting to the old behavior. I once had a habit of swearing. To change that habit, I asked my employees to notice when I swore and point it out to me each time. To monitor another habit, I paid one of my daughters 50 cents whenever she caught me driving without a seat belt. Getting this kind of cooperation from other people can assist you to change habits quickly as long you don't "kill the messenger"—that is, get angry with the person who's giving you the feedback.
- Assigning yourself a grade or a number to indicate how well you're doing at changing the habit. Once I chose to monitor my mood changes. I rated my moods on a scale of –10 (really depressed) to +10 (ecstatic) and entered these numbers several times on a day on a chart. Over a period of several weeks, I saw a distinct upswing in my moods.

Working with a client, the coach can invent many more ways to monitor their habit change. The point is to give people feedback about their progress. With an accurate and detailed feedback system, clients know when they're succeeding at instilling the new habit, and when they're not succeeding.

3. Practice, practice, practice—without reproach

This step is about graciousness. If we kick ourselves whenever we fail to perform a new behavior, we'll probably give up on the whole process of changing habits. A much kinder and more effective alternative is to simply notice when we get off track, renew our commitment to change, and practice the new behavior again and again—as many times as it takes to change the habit.

It's important for clients to remember this when they're disappointed with what they discover about themselves. One of my clients charted her self-esteem every day and her scores ranged from of –5 to –9 (indicating low self-esteem) for two weeks. In response to her reports of so many low scores, I said, "Congratulations! Now you've got a handle on this issue. And, you know that your self-esteem is not static. It can change." When clients begin to realize that they have some control over their habits, they can avoid being depressed about depression or unhappy about their unhappiness. When they remove that whole added layer of self-reproach, they can change habits with much less suffering and self-discipline.

The power of talking about new outcomes in our lives as a matter of changing habits is that it demystifies the outcomes and makes it easier to achieve them. Then the new outcomes that clients want are no longer blocked by a genetic defect. They're no longer blocked by an emotional disorder. They're no longer the result of cultural conditioning. Those new outcomes are as simple and doable as changing a habit. Maybe even the biggest changes in life can be as simple as learning to fasten a seatbelt or to stop biting fingernails. They're just habits.

4. Celebrate

Each time that you see progress in your movement toward developing the habit that you want, celebrate. Reward yourself when you notice changes and reward yourself when you have completed this process. The more appreciation you send your way, the more likely it is that the habit will change quickly and that the change will be permanent.

Once you change a habit in one area of life and celebrate it fully, you will be ready to take on new habits. Pretty soon, life will be different.

Handling emotions

Discharging emotions

One valuable benefit of life coaching occurs when we assist people to fully experience and discharge their emotions. I am confident in the benefit of emotional release because of something I've observed both in my clients and myself: Whatever we fully experience disappears. When we completely accept a negative feeling and permit ourselves to fully express it, then the feeling no longer has to dominate our thinking or compel our actions.

What's more, when we discharge emotions, all of a sudden we get much smarter. Our genius is often blocked by unexpressed emotions such as anger, sadness, embarrassment, hurt, and boredom. What conceals our true nature is layer upon layer of unreleased emotion. As those layers are removed, we can access our natural wisdom, compassion, creativity, and happiness.

I first encountered these ideas in the writing and teaching of Harvey Jackins who developed a technique called "Co-counseling" that specifically aims to help people discharge emotion. One of the fascinating phenomena Jackins describes is how emotion appears when people start to express it. For example, anger usually manifests as loud talking. Sadness manifests in crying. Embarrassment often shows up as laughter, and boredom is frequently revealed in animated talk. With any of these emotions, people can also experience shaking.

I see a direct overlap between the benefits of emotional discharge and the aims of life coaching. As clients access and release emotions at a deep level, they become more capable of solving their own problems. They can go from feeling angry and resentful to being loving and generous, from being upset and embarrassed to being creative and spontaneous. These shifts allow people to move into effective action.

You can help your clients experience the rewards of emotional release. This process does not require you to have training in counseling techniques. Begin by experimenting with these suggestions:

- *Provide a safe physical environment*—a place where clients can be free of interruptions. Also, choose a place where clients can weep openly, talk loudly, and laugh hysterically. Public places such as restaurants or office buildings seldom meet these criteria.

- *Provide a safe psychological environment.* Assure clients you will maintain confidentiality about their experiences with emotional release.

- *Invite emotional release* and give it full permission to occur. Remember that you don't have to use the more dramatic invitations, such as asking people to beat a pillow. (This is more of a therapeutic technique.) Instead, you can invite emotional release in a more casual way with comments such as, "You look angry. Tell me about it."

- *Ask people to repeat comments that seem to be filled with feeling* when you sense that it's appropriate. Repetition can promote emotional release.

- *Notice what stops emotional release.* When we talk too much or ask clients too many questions, we can interfere with their emotional discharge. For example, in order to answer the question "Why are you crying?", clients must stop crying. When we speak excessively, clients are cajoled into listening instead of emoting. Instead, listen even more intently than usual.

- *Just receive the client's emotion.* Don't give advice, share your own experiences, suggest problem-solving strategies, or even feed back the client's stated problem.

- *Notice specific behaviors that promote emotional release.* Most people find that full breathing allows emotional expression. If they hold their breath, it's difficult for people to shake, cry, or laugh. Sometimes holding a client's hand will also help. If you do this and notice that the client stops crying, then take your hand away.

- *Stay solid.* Avoid crying when clients cry. Focus on the client's experience, not your own feelings. What assists people while they discharge emotion is your steady, calm, and confident presence.

- *Give clients unconditional positive regard.* Commit to sending them your love, appreciation, joy, and respect, and as they receive these gifts they will often reward you with more emotional release.

Distinguishing attachment from preference

I find that much of the coaching I do is about helping clients make useful distinctions. For example, they can distinguish con-sulting from coaching, acceptance from resignation, and observations from interpretations. You can find other examples of key distinctions throughout this book.

Another distinction that your clients may find useful in handling emotions is the distinction between attachment and preference. Keep in mind that these two terms describe opposite ends of a con-tinuum; the difference between them is simply a matter of degree. At any given time, people can move closer to one end or another. When we assist clients to move toward the preference end of the continuum, we often promote their happiness.

Ken Keyes, author of *Handbook to Higher Consciousness*, defines an attachment as an emotionally backed demand. When I'm attached to something, then I demand to have it before I can feel satisfied; I simply will not be okay unless I get it or maintain it. In the previous sentence, the word it can refer to almost anything—a drug, a car, a house, a job, a relationship, an idea, a form of exercise, a goal, a sexual experience, or a level of income, to name a few examples. In extreme cases, as when people become addicted to a drug, they fear for their physical or emotional survival when the object of their addiction is missing.

Preferences represent a clear alternative to attachments. When we have a preference for something, we're able to say, "I want it—and I'll be okay even if I don't get it." Preferences are seldom backed with the kind of emotional force present in attachments. For example, if we don't get the job, car, or house we prefer, we might get upset, but we probably won't scream, shake, cry, feel afraid, or lose sleep over the loss.

Several years ago, I traveled to Amsterdam for a vacation with Trisha, my wife. Shortly after we arrived and were waiting in the Amsterdam airport, someone stole my laptop computer. When I discovered this, it took only a few seconds before I displayed the evidence of my emotionally backed demands: I swore. I yelled. For a few minutes, I couldn't even move. After a while, I stomped down the aisle to speak to a man behind the security counter, and I felt too upset to even give him my report. I was just not okay without my computer; I was definitely attached.

My friend Stan Lankowitz says that people are addicted to something when they repeatedly pursue the short-term, intense benefits of it in the face of great, longer-term pain and suffering. So, for example, people continue to drink even when that behavior leads to loss of their career and family. And people continue to smoke even when they're recovering from surgery for lung cancer.

With the passage of time, we can often move from a state of attachment to one of preference. For example, several hours after someone stole my computer in Amsterdam, I finally remembered that my happiness did not depend on having my computer. The next day, I was even able to enjoy my vacation with Trisha. I sure preferred not to lose my computer, but I was still okay without it.

As life coaches, we can create tremendous value for our clients by decreasing the amount of time it takes for them to move from attachment to preference. The following strategies can help.

SUGGEST THAT WE'RE MORE LIKELY TO KEEP OUR PREFERENCES
When we exist in a state of preference rather than attachment, we're more likely to get and keep what we want.

I reminded myself of this many times in the early days of College Survival, Inc., the company I founded. I believed that if I got attached to the success of the company, then it was more likely to fail. When I was able to stay lighthearted about the company's performance, I enjoyed my work more and I was able to take the kind of risks that allowed the company to succeed and grow.

I take the same attitude toward my marriage. I am deeply in love with Trisha, and more than almost anything else I want this relationship to continue. But if I ever become attached to this relationship, I'll probably stop doing the things that preserve it—for example, speaking candidly and fully expressing my emotions. Ironically, maintaining my marriage sometimes means being willing to act in ways that put the relationship at risk.

ALLOW FULL SELF-EXPRESSION
When we fully permit and fully experience any unpleasant feeling, it tends to lose its power over us. With this in mind, we can let clients talk about their attachments until their emotionally backed demands start to soften. This strategy is especially useful when we refrain from giving advice or trying to solve clients' problems.

When my computer was stolen, Trisha granted me a huge gift by allowing me to fully express my emotions about this event. She just let me discharge all my feelings about the loss. She didn't say, "Now, calm down, Dave; it's really not that bad," or, "Why are you so upset? It's just a computer, and it can be replaced." Once I vented my feelings, I found it much easier to move from attachment to preference.

WORRY THE ATTACHMENT TO DEATH

Ask clients to describe the worst possible thing that could happen if they lose the object or circumstance of their attachment. When they're able to imagine this worst possible event and accept it, then they've moved a significant distance toward a state of preference.

This line of thinking really helped me when my computer was stolen. Soon after I discovered it was missing, I asked myself what was the worst thing that could result from this incident. My answer was that someone could take all the personal journals I kept on that computer and send them to my local newspaper, *The Rapid City Journal*. Still, I doubted that the *Journal* would publish those journals. Even if they were published, I saw that I'd be embarrassed and perhaps have a few law-suits on my hands. And, I knew I could create and maintain a wonderful life even if these things happened.

UNCOVER THE EGO EQUATION AND ERASE IT

When clients are attached, the coach can assist them to uncover the equation that underlies the attachment. Becoming fully conscious of that equation is a big step toward changing the equation and releasing the attachment.

For instance, when a client is attached to a car, then the implied ego equation is I = MY CAR. If this client is involved in a traffic accident and the car is damaged or destroyed, then the client could feel personally damaged or destroyed. Describing the attachment in such broad and obvious terms can quickly assist the client to see the costs of the attachment.

When those costs become clear, then clients can take an even more liberating step and erase the ego equation. They can see that they are more than their car, more than their computer, more than their job, and more than their marriage. They could lose any of these things and fairly quickly be just fine. When they accept this insight, clients can discover a happiness that does not depend on external circumstances. That's the power of preference.

Speaking with self-responsibility

There's power in using "I-messages" as a tool for speaking with greater self-awareness and personal responsibility, and this tool remains largely under-used.

Many people in the helping professions are already familiar with the term *I-messages*. Even so, this term could be new to many of your clients, and you may find it useful to teach I-messages in detail.

Begin with basic distinctions

These are some points I often find useful in introducing the concept of I-messages:

- *I-messages are less likely to generate defensiveness in others.* For example, most people will find it easier to hear, "I noticed your time sheet was late after I asked for it three times," rather than, "You're irresponsible with time sheets." In a similar way, "I've really been tired at night and I've been doing a lot of the cooking" will probably create a different reaction in others than, "You never help me with the cooking."

- *A primary value of I-messages is that they allow us to be self-generative*—to take responsibility for our thoughts, feelings, words, and actions.

- *You-messages are, in many ways, the opposite of I-messages.* You-messages tend to blame, label, and judge people. In addition, You-messages are often filled with the language of obligation—statements that include phrases such as *you should.* For example: "You're not an effective leader and you should be a lot better at this by now."

- Besides being easier for other people to receive than You-messages, *I-messages are often easier for us to send.* Speaking with I-messages in a timely fashion prevents us from "stuffing" our feelings and allowing unspoken upsets to accumulate.

Despite these potential benefits, your clients can find I-messages tough to master, even when these people have the best of intentions.

I find that it often helps to list five basic elements of an I-message. The first three of these elements I consider essential. The last two are optional, and I recommend using them with caution.

Describe observations

We can start I-messages with a statement of what we observe—"just the facts, ma'am," not an interpretation of the facts. For instance, "You did not return my last three calls" states a verifiable fact. "You're arrogant" is an evaluation of those facts, and it may not be the most accurate interpretation.

When stating observations, our task is sticking to what we see and hear. A useful guideline is to think of observations as being what a video camera and microphone would record.

It's possible to send an I-message even when we don't have specific observations to offer. When this is true, we can state our interpretation or judgment and label it as such. For example: "My interpretation is that you're angry with me." Or, "Right now I think that you're ready to fire me."

The difference between observations and interpretation is not absolute. This distinction points to a continuum, not a dichotomy. Some statements combine elements of interpretation and observation.

Describe feelings

Adding the dimension of feelings often adds emotional impact to an I-message. Though this might sound obvious, many people who want to state their feelings actually end up sharing their thoughts and interpretations instead.

Remember that feelings include basic emotions such as anger, sadness, and fear: "I feel afraid" is part of an I-message that reveals a feeling. The statement "I feel like we're not getting along" seems to refer to an emotion but actually reveals an interpretation.

To increase your level of self-responsibility, leave out words such as *because* or *whenever* in reference to your feelings. These words tend to blame others for the way we feel. An example is, "I felt angry because you were late for our session." Feeling angry is only one possible reaction we can have when someone is late. It's usually more accurate and self-empowering to say, "You were late for the session, and I'm feeling angry."

State what you want

A third useful element you can add to I-messages is a statement of what you want. Often this means including phrases such as *I want*, *I request that*, and *I'd like you to*.

Statements about what you want are usually more useful when you request an observable behavior: "Please be on time for the session" is more effective than "Please alter the context of the space you're coming from about our sessions."

Two more elements to use cautiously

Stating what you think can sometimes enhance an I-message. For instance, "I fear for our relationship and I think we could both gain from seeing a marriage counselor." Be careful, however, since the words *I think* can easily lead to judgment or interpretation.

You could also state your intention: "I fear for our relationship, and I intend to get counseling." When used inappropriately, intentions can sound like threats and generate defensiveness in other people: "If you don't come with me to see a marriage counselor, then I intend to file for a divorce."

Beware of You-messages even when they're positive

Positive You-messages can lead to as much mischief as other types of You-messages. By positive You-messages I mean statements such as, "You're a brilliant coach" or, "You're such a good boy."

The problem with such statements is that they can leave listeners confused about what you specifically appreciate. To avoid this problem, you could say, "I heard you come up with 18 solutions to that problem and I feel excited about that" instead of, "You're a brilliant coach." You could also say, "Son, I saw that you kept your clothes off the floor and made your bed, and I really like that" instead of, "You're such a good boy."

Improving relationships
Recreating the experience of another person

With some assistance from us, our clients can recreate their experience of a friend, coworker, child, spouse, parent, or other key person in their lives. The exercise I'm about to describe exists for this purpose. While it works for people who are in significant conflict, this exercise can also benefit people when their relationships are going well. When it comes to experiencing joy, intimacy, and mutual contribution, there's no upper limit to the value we can create through our relationships.

This exercise consists of six questions for your client to answer. He can respond verbally, in writing, or in both ways. Before you begin, ask him to choose one person to focus on for the entire exercise.

I've done this exercise many times, so I will provide an example by answering questions about my own relationship with Muhammad Yunus, who has been introduced as "the person who has done more to eliminate poverty than anyone in history." Yunus founded the Grameen Bank, which aims to eliminate abject poverty in the world through microcredit—making very small loans, usually to women.

1. How do you automatically and unconsciously relate to this person?

In other words, when you're not being thoughtful, who is this person in your life? What assumptions do you make about who this person is?

For instance, in my initial meetings with Yunus, I assumed him to be a brilliant person who was busy and largely unavailable. I also saw him as someone to be revered and not approachable as a potential friend.

2. Who are you in the presence of that person?

Generally, who are you around that person? What do you feel? How do you act? Who do you see yourself to be?

Early in my relationship with Yunus, I saw myself as young and inexperienced. I acted simply as man who provided money for his work. In other words, I saw myself as not being up to much.

3. What's your unconscious purpose in being with this person?

Another way to ask this question is, "Why do I now spend time with this person?"

Initially, my purpose around Yunus was just to be social—to make small talk and maybe handle a few details about the fund-raising project we were doing together.

Once your client has answered the first three questions about his automatic behavior, he can begin to create a new relationship with the following questions.

4. Who are you willing to create this person to be?

Who could you imagine this person to be, and are you willing to let him or her actually be this person?

In my own case, I was willing for Yunus to be interested in me, curious about me, and hungry to learn what I know. I also became willing to see him as my partner in creating projects to end abject poverty in the world. I could even create him to be somebody who is thrilled to see me.

5. WHO ARE YOU WILLING TO CREATE YOURSELF TO BE WHEN YOU'RE
   WITH THIS PERSON?

When relating to Yunus, I was willing to see myself as a top-notch life coach. I could also create myself to be an equal partner with Yunus, a true friend, and someone with whom he could have a lot of fun.

6. WHAT ARE YOU WILLING TO CREATE AS YOUR PURPOSE WHEN YOU'RE
   WITH THIS PERSON?

Instead of acting on a purpose to share small talk and handle a few details with Yunus, I saw that with him I could adopt a purpose to alter the quality of life on earth while celebrating our friendship.

What's happened to me has been no less than a miracle every time I've done this exercise. In this particular case, I moved from being a young kid with an "aw, shucks" attitude around Yunus, to someone who could stand with him as a full partner in projects with global impact. And since making these shifts in my perception of both Yunus and myself, my personal and professional relationship with him has changed dramatically, moving much closer to the new purposes I created for being with him.

When you first present this exercise, some clients might object that it all takes place "just in your mind." Well, of course. For me, that's the whole point: powerful coaching assists us to rearrange our mind—to release the unconscious assumptions, beliefs, and purposes that limit our vision of ourselves and other people. When we consciously release those artificial obstacles to our brilliance and personal power, we create a whole new way of being in the world.

Receiving compliments

It's socially acceptable for people to deflect compliments. This kind of deflection shows up in client comments such as:

- "Oh, you say that to everyone."
- "You're my life coach. Of course, you see me as wonderful."
- "You're always optimistic. You find the silver lining in every cloud."
- "You just say that about me because I pay you."

This pervasive habit of deflecting compliments cheats clients out of experiencing their personal power and brilliance and often prevents relationships from moving to a deeper level of intimacy. When clients deflect our compliments, they are, in a sense, resisting appreciation and love—an experience that can frustrate any friend or life coach.

POINT OUT ANY PATTERN OF DEFLECTING COMPLIMENTS

Once clients become aware of a this habit, they're one step closer to changing it. You can serve clients by pointing out their pattern of deflecting compliments whenever it occurs in the coaching session. In addition, you can explore whether this pattern persists outside of the coaching session.

OFFER SPECIFIC COMPLIMENTS

One way to assist clients in accepting compliments is to speak specifically. When clients don't take a compliment to heart, we're often speaking in terms that are too general. So instead of saying, "You look great," you can tell a client, "I appreciate the fact that you're smiling a lot." Or, instead of saying, "You're really creative today," you can say, "I just heard you say five solutions to this problem that you've never said before today."

REPEAT THE COMPLIMENT

You can take a cue from the people who create advertisements and harness the power of repetition: keep giving the compliment until the client no longer deflects it. You can even announce your intention: "I will keep saying this until I sense that you've fully received my compliment."

ASK CLIENTS TO RECEIVE THE COMPLIMENT

Simply asking clients to receive your compliments can work wonders. Just say, "I want to offer you a compliment, and my request is that you just listen to it and receive it."

A related option is to give clients some brief instruction on ways to receive compliments. For example: "When I compliment you today, you can experiment with several responses. One is to just say 'Thanks.' Another is to say, 'Thank you. You're very perceptive.' Or, you can say nothing at all."

PRE-ANSWER THE OBJECTION

As you get to know clients, you can often anticipate their possible objections to your compliments. Then you can answer those objections at the same time you offer your compliments: "Now, you might be thinking I'm saying this because you're paying me to support you as a life coach. I assure you that my intention is to speak candidly, and I will compliment you only when it represents my authentic experience of you in the moment."

Using success strategies

A skilled life coach—and a skilled client—is someone who looks at process as well as content. That's an unusual ability. Most people don't even make the distinction between content and process.

Content is mostly about *what*—what subjects to learn, what investments to buy, what goals to set, what kind of exercise to do, what kind of foods to eat, what habits to adopt. But process is about *how*—how we learn any subject, how we choose to spend our money, how we maintain any exercise program, how we change any habit, or meet any goal.

While mastery of a particular content area is a primary characteristic of a consultant, mastery of many processes is a fundamental part of being a skilled life coach.

In my life coaching work, I find myself drawing on a core set of processes that apply across the board to any content, any change in thinking or behavior that clients want to make. I call them *Power Processes* or *Success Strategies*. These strategies distill the essence of what I've learned about personal growth and spiritual transformation. I've constantly searched for ways to express these ideas in language that is easily understood and in ways that the ideas will be used.

Following are brief summaries of each Power Process as it is described in more detail in my books *Creating Your Future* and *Human Being*. Following these summaries is a summary of the 12 Success Strategies that are described in detail in my book, *Falling Awake*.

Summary of the Power Processes

1. **Determine what you want.** When your daily activities and choices are guided by a clear vision for the future, you can be more effective.
2. **Survey your life.** Being honest about your effectiveness in many areas unleashes a powerful force for change.
3. **Practice acceptance.** One way to solve a problem is to begin by loving it.
4. **Examine moment-to-moment choices.** Remembering that genius is in the detail, you can treat the small choices with care and watch your whole life start to change.

5. **Investigate your role.** In any situation, you can ask, "How have I created this?" and "How can I turn this around?"

6. **Focus your attention.** Learning to "be here now" releases mental distractions and increases your effectiveness at any activity.

7. **Manage your interpretations.** The ways you choose to interpret your circumstances could instantly bring you closer to the life of your dreams.

8. **Speak candidly.** When you express yourself fully, you can make a loving contribution to yourself and others.

9. **Make and keep promises.** By making promises to yourself and others, you can re-create your life and move into action.

10. **Surrender and trust.** A powerful way to deal with people and events is to stop futile attempts to control them.

11. **Persist.** When faced with a problem, you can keep looking for answers beyond the first good solution that occurs to you, and you can stay in this inquiry until you have developed at least seven solutions. Only then, go into action.

12. **Notice your expectations.** When you become aware of expectations, you discover a major source of upset—and ways to create happiness.

13. **Listen fully.** Listening can be a whole way of life, an activity that affects everything you do.

14. **Enjoy and celebrate.** In almost any situation, even the most difficult, you can find a source of delight.

15. **Detach and play full out.** You can fully involve yourself in the people and projects in your life, even as you stay loose and lighthearted.

16. **Choose your conversations and your community.** To fulfill your goals, take part in conversations and hang around the people who are aligned with your purpose, plans, and values.

17. **Revise your habits.** You can improve your life quickly when you see faults as habits instead of personal defects.

18. **Appreciate mistakes.** When you know ways to learn from them, mistakes can be powerful and patient teachers.

19. **Think clearly.** Rather than going through your daily routine on automatic pilot, you can be thoughtful and use simple techniques of logic to move directly toward the life of your dreams.

20. **Act courageously.** Fears need not stop you from doing what you've chosen to do.

21. **Manage your associations**. When you link a desired new behavior to pleasure, you can establish it with a minimum of struggle.

22. **Contribute.** Assisting others to get what they want and taking on bigger problems are ways to create a wonderful life for yourself.

23. **Define your values, align your actions.** Personal effectiveness includes being clear about your fundamental values and making choices consistent with them.

Summary of the Success Strategies

1. **Determine what you want.** Trust your desires and create a bold, detailed vision for your future.

2. **Tell the truth.** Speak candidly, make promises, and align your actions with your words.

3. **Move toward love.** Be willing to release antagonism, and embrace problems as a step toward solving them.

4. **Take responsibility.** In any situation, ask "How did I create this?" and "How can I create a new result?"

5. **Lighten your load.** Move toward bliss by letting go of your attachments and expectations, and by choosing new ways to manage distress.

6. **Focus your awareness.** Release mental distractions and pay exquisite attention to moment-to-moment choices.

7. **Listen fully.** Open up to receiving any messages—compliments, criticism, or whatever the world is sending you in the moment.

8. **Choose your conversations.** Understand the role of conversations in creating your world, and center conversations with care.

9. **Change your habits.** Take the mystery out of personal transformation by following three simple steps to make consistent changes in your behavior.

10. **Persist.** When faced with a problem, look beyond the first solutions that occur to you, and stay in action until you get what you want.

11. **Contribute.** As you get more of what you want in life, find added joy by assisting others to get what *they* want.

12. **Celebrate.** Constantly notice what you enjoy about your life right now, and go for fun.

Chapter Six
Professional Issues for Life Coaches

Developing appropriate intimacy with clients

Aim for balance

My commitment to the people I coach is to love them according to a dictionary definition of that word—to hold them in "high regard and profound affection." This is intimacy.

However, as coaches we can be intimate in a way that creates discomfort for clients. When that happens, we've made a mistake. The way we touch or make eye contact, the subjects we discuss, the way we express emotion—any of these things can frighten or confuse people and even chase them away.

It's also possible to not be intimate enough with clients—to be aloof and distant. When we withhold too much of what we're thinking and feeling, we fail to create a sacred space, one in which the miracles of life coaching can occur. Then clients might back off and avoid coming out to share that space with us.

When I notice any of the following, I examine whether I have been intimate enough in the life coaching relationship:

- *My client is aloof.* The client discusses only professional issues.
- *I start to focus on my performance as a life coach*, not on serving the client.

- *My client never complains*. When people periodically complain
  that the coaching is getting a little too intense and a little too intimate, then I'm probably on track. If the client hasn't complained
  that I am being too intimate, then it might be time for me to
  speak more candidly. Of course, different people have different
  tolerances for intimacy and different boundaries. When some
  clients complain that it's too intimate, it may be that you have
  gone over the line and it is time to back off.

Ask for permission to be candid

One way to discover an appropriate level of intimacy with each
client is to check with the client.

For instance, you could say: "I am here to assist you, to empower
you, and to help you in any way I can to have the most wonderful
life possible. I think it would be valuable to talk about your alcohol
use. Are you willing?" You can even suggest that clients not answer
the question immediately. Give them the option to return to the
question at a later session.

This approach reinforces your purpose in life coaching and
gives the client permission to choose the level of intimacy in the
interaction.

Assume a certain level of intimacy

You can also just assume a certain level of intimacy. For example,
over the last few years, my wife and I have been coached about
sexuality. The couple who provides this coaching is so frank that
we have often been surprised but not offended. These people
talk about the most intimate details of sex much like I would talk
about my portable telephone. But, they speak in such an easy and
matter-of-fact way that so far I have never been insulted.

Say that I have some hard feedback for a client, such as "Your
breath smells," or "It's hard for me when you are late for a session."

Given my commitment to the client, I can say these things out of a spirit of partnership and love. When I do, even in our very first meeting, clients are likely to perceive that love. If they don't, I can apologize and let them know that I did not intend to insult or offend them.

There's an old saying about a true diplomat: She can tell an employee that he's fired, and he'll walk away saying thanks. In a similar way, you can often give people difficult feedback, ask probing questions, and talk about intimate topics and simply assume that it's all okay. And, most of the time it *will* be just fine with your clients.

Dealing with sexual attraction

You might feel sexual attraction toward a client, or a client might express sexual attraction to you. If sexual feelings arise, you can respond in some of the following ways.

ACKNOWLEDGE AND AFFIRM
Some possible responses to sexual feelings that arise during a life coaching session are to judge, deny, or repress them. Those responses have the potential to increase the force of sexual feelings, interfering with the life coaching process.

Instead of repression, you can acknowledge and even celebrate the fact that people are sexual beings. So if clients ever say, "I really find you attractive," you can thank them for being so honest and remind them that this type of authenticity is one way to get the most from life coaching.

You might even affirm them with, "It is understandable that you might have these feelings given the very intimate things that we have discussed."

If you are experiencing feelings of sexual attraction toward your client, this is one area where I recommend against full disclosure. Far too often a client could misinterpret your disclosure as an advance. I recommend that you deal with these feeling with a life coach mentor or psychologist.

SEPARATE SEX FROM INTIMACY

In our society, people often equate intimacy with sex. Many of the times when we have intimate feelings are also times when we have sexual feelings.

There is intimacy—deep sharing and full self-disclosure—in the life coaching relationship. People sometimes forget that we can separate this kind of intimacy from sex. You can remind your clients of this distinction to help eliminate misunderstandings.

Hand holding, hugging, and other forms of touching are not necessarily sexual. As long as clients are comfortable with them, these forms of physical contact can be a part of life coaching—even in this age of sexual harassment lawsuits. If you are in doubt about the message that your touch is sending to your client, check it out. For example, you might say to your client, "When you were crying about your father's death, I held your hand for a short time. My intention was to provide comfort and empathy. Were you comfortable with that? Or did I overstep your boundaries?"

SAY WHAT YOU'RE *NOT* SAYING

One strategy for clear communication in any emotionally charged situation is to say what you are *not* saying. If you love your client, you can say that. Then you can rule out the possibility of a sexual relationship.

Suppose you tell a client that you love her. The client might unconsciously add something to your message: *My coach loves me and wants to have sex with me.* To prevent that misunderstanding, you could say, "I really think you're a wonderful person. I am *not* saying that I want to be sexually intimate with you."

RULE OUT SEX

A related strategy is to state clearly that there is no chance that you will have a sexual relationship with your clients. You don't have to belittle a client if she makes an advance, but you can say, "Thank you. But sex is never going to happen in this relationship. No chance."

While ruling out sex, you can repeat your commitment to the client: "I appreciate your honesty in saying how you feel about me. I just want you to know that I'm committed to empowering you in every way I can. Part of that commitment is that I would never be sexually intimate with you."

You can even have this be part of the initial conversation that you have with your clients. Recently, when I started coaching an attractive woman, I told her that although our relationship would be very open, I did not want it to include any flirtation.

GET COACHING MENTORING

Sometimes feeling sexual toward a client gets in the way when you want to be a great coach. If this happens, get some assistance. Find someone you trust to help you with your coaching.

HELP THE CLIENT FIND ANOTHER COACH

I don't think there's anything wrong with sex, and I don't even think there's anything wrong with even feeling sexual toward a client. But, there are times when it's hard to make the life coaching relationship work, even if you use all the strategies listed above. When the issue of sex becomes too distracting for you or for your client, then it may be time for you to help your client find another coach.

Handling dual relationships

Dual relationships take place when you have an additional relationship with a client beyond that of a life coach. For instance, you could coach someone who is also your employee or employer. Dual relationships can also surface when you use life coaching skills with your own family members and friends.

Handling dual relationships can be tricky. In these situations, it's hard for a life coach to be agenda free. Sometimes there is a power imbalance, as when an employer coaches an employee. And, coaching becomes complicated when added responsibilities are present: As a parent, I have a responsibility to see that my child behaves in a certain way. As an employer, I have a responsibility to see that my employees get certain tasks done.

Among psychotherapists, there is a code of ethics that prohibits dual relationships. Counseling people such as friends, employees, or family members is considered unethical. I think this is a wonderful principle for counselors, but I don't think that is necessary for life coaches. In my own work, for example, I've seen lots of good happen when I coach employees and when employees coach me.

To prevent problems that can arise from dual relationships, first recognize when they occur. Then you can clearly choose what to do next.

Acknowledge the danger

Before you enter into a dual relationship as a life coach, acknowledge the danger. Tell the person you're coaching that you want to experiment with having a dual relationship for a while. Also, point out the potential problems, including power imbalance and the presence of conflicting agendas. Assist clients to enter a dual relationship consciously, and only enter into such a relationship with the client's full consent.

Ensure that there's a demand for coaching

One way to prevent the dangers of dual relationships is to ensure that the client has a huge appetite for coaching. I won't coach employees, family members, or close friends unless they repeatedly request it. I don't want an employee to ask for coaching in order to get points, or friends to ask for coaching out of a sense that they owe me a favor. When someone really wants my coaching, then I can usually trust that they're making the request without an ulterior motive.

Limit the coaching

You can sometimes avoid the dangers of dual relationships by choosing to limit the scope of the coaching. While coaching an employee, you could choose to work only with his health-related goals—but not, for example, the employee's career goals. That avoids the kind of awkwardness that can develop when employees come to you for coaching about salary negotiation or career changes.

Bracket your coaching

A related option is to bracket the times when your role switches from that of being a coach. Create a clear demarcation between roles and announce which role you intend to operate from at any given moment. You can do this through comments such as:

- "I've got something I could teach you here about ways to handle your investments. If you're interested in pursuing this, then I am no longer acting as your life coach but as a financial advisor."
- "I'm willing to coach you about making a career change. If I do, I'll be stepping out of my role as your employer."
- "I'm trained as a psychotherapist, so we could shift from life coaching at this point and talk about dealing with a possible mental disorder."

The key is to have your role as a coach out on the table. Acknowledge when you're coaching and when you're not. Point out when your role switches from coach to friend, relative, manager, counselor, consultant, or something else. To promote clarity, keep reminding clients of this point.

When appropriate, release your agenda

At College Survival, Inc., we had effectiveness coaches whose role was to help each employee get what he or she wanted in life. This coaching was provided as an employee benefit, like disability coverage and health insurance. My direction to each coach was to help employees get whatever they wanted, even if employees concluded that they wanted to leave the company. I felt so strongly about the value of coaching that I was willing to lose employees.

Look to see whether you have an agenda for your client before entering into a dual relationship. Then ask yourself if you're willing to modify or release that agenda. If you're not, then refer the client to another coach.

Review your clients

Talk about your clients with another life coach or mentor when you suspect that a dual relationship might be a problem. Sometimes other people will see a dual relationship problem where you do not.

You can also learn more about boundary issues and dual relationships through professional coaching organizations and books. One practical guide is *Tangled Relationships: Managing Boundary Issues in the Human Services* by Frederic G. Reamer.

Making referrals to other professionals

At times, the most contributing thing we can do for our client is to refer him to another professional. That professional could be a physician, a mental health professional, lawyer, accountant, or a consultant.

When choosing when and how to refer, we can quickly run into many gray areas. Making this choice is an art, not a science.

One path to clarity is to use your intuition. When it's time to refer a client, you'll probably know in your heart and soul. As soon as you raise the question, then it's time to look to some of the following options.

Consider your range of knowledge and skill

Choices about referrals depend partially on your skills and subject matter expertise. I used to work as an accountant, so I can coach clients about accounting, and I may not refer clients to an accountant as soon as other life coaches would. However, I have no training or qualification to advise people on treating mental disorders. So if one of my clients is struggling with severe or long-term depression, I'll refer this person to a psychiatrist.

Sometimes I'll continue to coach the people I refer to others, as long as they continue to see that other professional about a specific problem. For instance, I could continue to coach someone with depression, as long as that person is following his psychiatrist's treatment plan.

When appropriate, I will request permission to talk to the other professionals involved so that we can coordinate our efforts.

Refer in cases of serious illness

I usually don't want to coach people with a serious mental illness unless they're getting professional help. That's true when a client is dealing with a condition described in the *Diagnostic and Statistical Manual of Mental Disorders*, published by the American Psychiatric Association.

I take a similar approach when clients have a life-threatening health problem. For example, I would be happy to coach people who are getting hospice care as long as these people are taking care of themselves in an appropriate way.

When you refer a client, you could continue life coaching and set appropriate boundaries:

- *Declare certain topics to be off limits*: "I think that any conversation about your past with that person needs to be done with a therapist. I won't have this conversation with you anymore, but I'm still willing to coach you in other areas." If a person has or is dealing with a certain topic in therapy, then you probably don't want deal with it as a life coach.
- *Declare certain methods off limits*: "Emotional release is part of my work with some clients, but it's not going to be part of our coaching. I think emotional release is something you need to do with a therapist."
- *Do both of the above*: "We are not going to talk about that issue, nor are we going to use the process of emotional release on any topic."

Refer when clients stop making healthy choices

When it looks like clients are no longer making healthy life choices, then it's time to reassess your coaching relationship. Refer them when, from an ethical point of view, you can no longer tolerate their behavior.

For example, one of my clients just kept telling me how depressed she was. I asked her repeatedly how she intended to handle that. She agreed several times to see a therapist but never did. Finally, she started taking Prozac that had been prescribed for her brother but she still hadn't seen a doctor. When I discovered this, I said I was not willing to coach her unless she took her problem to an appropriate expert.

Continue coaching until the problem reaches a certain level

When I was president of College Survival, Inc., we offered coaching to our employees. One of our guidelines was that we would continue to coach an employee about a problem until the problem reached a certain level of severity. For example, if the problem led to physical symptoms such as loss of sleep or loss of appetite and/or lasted more than three months, then we saw it as beyond the scope of coaching.

Create your own guidelines about when to refer people. Consider putting these guidelines in writing. You could include them in a life coaching agreement that you ask people to sign before you start coaching them.

Negotiate for an assessment

When clients resist a referral to a therapist, you can suggest that they just get an assessment: "I don't know about mental disorders, and maybe things really are okay with you. But I don't want to proceed with this coaching until you get a therapist's opinion."

This is the approach I've taken with two clients when I was concerned about their possible chemical dependency. "I don't know if you are an alcoholic or a drug addict," I said. "But I have enough concern that I want you to get some professional assessment before we continue to work together."

It's possible to share this kind of concern in a non-judgmental way. You can just say that you're concerned about a problem that falls outside of your expertise. State that you're requesting a referral out of your commitment to the client's personal and professional effectiveness.

Choose when to coach people who are taking psychiatric medications

One of the guidelines that I have is to not coach people who need to be medicated for psychological reasons. This is a guideline, not a firm rule. Though I want to be cautious, there are circumstances where it makes sense for me to coach such people.

My overall goal is to be sure that these clients are clear about the boundaries between life coaching and therapy. I don't want people to use life coaching as a substitute for medication or therapy, and I include this point in the life coaching agreement that all of my clients sign. I suggest that you choose your guidelines in this area and state them up front.

A final option is to stop coaching the client. I choose this option when I'm clear that life coaching is not producing value for the client.

Choose your place on the referral continuum

How we refer people can be just as crucial as *when* we refer them. When looking at the process of making a referral, I see a continuum of possibilities:

- *Suggest a referral*: "One possibility would be for you to see a lawyer about this."
- *Give an assignment*: "As your homework before our next session, I'd like you to choose about seeing a lawyer."
- *Negotiate*: "I want to list a couple of possibilities for therapists you could see and choose which possibility works for you and me."
- *Insist*: "I will not continue working with you until you see a doctor to get treatment about hypertension. Please promise me that you will do this before the next time we get together."

At the high end of this spectrum, I'm just giving an option. When descending the spectrum to the level of insisting, I find that making choices about referrals gets harder.

One thing that influences my choice is the degree of the problem. Suppose that a client has a question about tax planning. We brainstorm some options for getting an answer, such as consulting an accountant or talking to someone at the IRS. Eventually, the client agrees to go to an accountant. Over our next five sessions, this client keeps promising to see an accountant and never does. In this situation, I am not going to insist on the referral. But if I find out that he hasn't paid taxes for the last five years, I'll shift from giving options to giving an assignment or negotiating.

Compared to some life coaches, I'm more likely to continue with clients who consistently break their agreements. Even when clients' behavior has serious potential consequences, I usually see my job as *assisting* them rather than *insisting* that they follow through on a commitment. I think people learn wonderful lessons when they experience significant consequences.

Responding to illegal or unethical activity

Imagine that one of your clients says, "I've never told anybody this, but I stole about $30,000 from my employer last year and never got caught. I feel guilty, and I don't know what to do about it."

Or your client says, "I'm very worried about my level of debt, but I think I can solve the problem by embezzling from my employer."

Or, what if another client says: "I sexually molested a neighbor's four-year-old girl. I'm so ashamed. I just don't know what came over me."

And another might say, "I run a big company. I have a wonderful life and a wonderful family, including four children. And about 30 years ago I killed someone while driving drunk. No one ever found out about this. I've been sober for 25 years, but I still feel terrible. I want to get past this incident and get on with my life."

Faced with such hypothetical examples, some new life coaches might say, "Come on, we're working with basically healthy, normal, and competent people. These kinds of things are not going to happen with our clients."

Well, some of my clients have reported such things to me. On three occasions I've had clients admit illegal activities, including theft and tax evasion.

This issue is incredibly complex, and we can't pretend to know all the answers. Imagine that you could have coached Thomas Jefferson shortly before he signed the Declaration of Independence. You could have said, "Tom, you know, you're contemplating an illegal activity. As your coach, I'm going to report you if you insist on pursuing this unlawful deed." Keep in mind that the people who signed this Declaration not only knew they were breaking the law— they also believed that they were signing their death certificate. (And, many were.)

Consider some current and perhaps less dramatic examples: A client confesses that she habitually drives 30 miles an hour over the highway speed limit. Another person reports that he's sold marijuana and still occasionally uses it. A third client reveals that he failed to file a tax return last year.

Life coaching is about promoting the client's agenda. Sometimes that agenda might include an illegal activity and/or actions that you consider unethical. When choosing how to respond, you face a lot of gray areas. Your options include keeping the activity confidential, encouraging the client to handle the problem, calling the police, ending the life coaching relationship, and more.

Know the applicable laws

You can begin by consulting an attorney for state laws that could affect your work as a life coach. Remember that these laws usually apply to other helping professionals, including physicians and psychotherapists. There are few if any laws that apply specifically to life coaches. But you could still be held legally accountable in certain cases, probably to the laws that apply to counselors and psychotherapists.

When you ask about how those laws affect life coaches, you could get a complex and even confusing interpretation. Some topics to investigate include:

- The kinds of communication with your clients that are considered to be privileged.

- Circumstances where you could be arrested for harboring a criminal, concealing evidence, or aiding and abetting a crime.
- Circumstances where you might be considered in contempt of court for withholding information about a client.
- When might you be required by law to report illegal activities?

I have done this research with my attorney in the state of South Dakota, and I was surprised at what I discovered. Each state/country is different, even each attorney will offer different interpretations, and I encourage you to find out more about the laws in your local area. In addition to attorneys, you might find that professional associations for life coaches or counselors are also useful sources of help with this issue.

Declare up front what you will keep confidential

During your first session with a client, lay out your ground rules about which activities you will keep confidential. Put these rules in writing and discuss them with clients.

My life coaching agreement currently includes this statement:

I (the client) understand that confidentiality in the life coaching relationship is limited. Confidentiality will not apply to certain crimes that have been committed or certain crimes that are being planned. Such crimes may need to be reported to legal authorities. It is also possible that certain topics could be reviewed with other life coaching professionals for training and development purposes.

This is just one example of how to explain confidentiality to clients. You could also say any of the following:

"I want you to know that we have a confidential relationship except in a few areas. If you tell me that you've committed a felony or that you're about to commit a felony, I will report that to the police."

"This is a totally confidential relationship. You can tell me anything, and my lips are sealed. Even if I'm taken to court to testify against you, I won't reveal anything you tell me. I'll keep your confidences even if it means going to jail."

"If you tell me that you have broken the law or are planning a crime, I might report you to the police. Some illegal activities I will report; others I won't. My choice will be based on the seriousness of the crime, when it was committed, the consequences of the crime, and the possible consequences to you and your family of reporting the crime."

"If you tell me that you've committed or are planning to commit an act that I consider unethical, I might choose to end the life coaching relationship. I might end the relationship even if the act is technically legal, or if the act is illegal and remains undetected."

Of course, I can't give you the answers to questions about handling your clients' illegal or unethical activities. I can only invite you to arrive at these answers for yourself with guidance from your lawyer—and your conscience. My choice about handling illegal or unethical activity is usually to follow my conscience first, but I also want to know enough about the law so I don't end up in prison.

Life is complicated, and life coaching can get you into some complicated situations. I urge you to inquire thoroughly into this issue of confidentiality and inform your clients of your policies. Know your options and your values before you are faced with legal problems.

Continuing professional development

Continuing education and training is important for professionals in any area—education, law, medicine, and others. Life coaches can also adopt this commitment.

One quality of a master life coach is a passion for personal and professional development. We can transform ourselves in a way that promotes transformation in our clients.

When we hear about professional development, many of us think first about taking workshops, reading books, listening to tapes, or even learning to pray and meditate. These are all great options, and following are three more.

Review your clients

For life coaches, one key tool is reviewing our clients—getting coaching or mentoring about our coaching. We can debrief with other life coaches about our interaction with a client and then consider their suggestions for ways to move ahead with that client. One benefit of this review is that we can quickly expand our kit of coaching tools and techniques. In addition, we take on the role of a client for a while and experience the power of receiving coaching as well as giving it.

Take breaks

Every time the heart beats, it takes a momentary break before it beats again. When we breathe, there's a pause between an exhalation and the next inhalation. We can mirror this wisdom of nature and enhance our effectiveness by taking periodic breaks from coaching. Call these breaks anything you want—sabbaticals, down time, vacations, or mental health days. We can all use them to rest, rejuvenate, and sustain the energy level needed for effective coaching.

You can take these breaks in the spirit of service to your clients. Let them know well ahead of time that you're planning a vacation. If you're taking a long break, you could refer clients to a substitute life coach for that period. I know a very successful life coach who is committed to one week off a month.

Get your own life coach

Experiencing life coaching for yourself will improve your ability to provide life coaching in several ways.

One way is that life coaching allows you to go deeper within yourself. As you unleash more insights about your own way of being in the world, uncover your brilliance, and take action to raise the quality of your life, you become more effective in assisting clients to unleash *their* insights, uncover their brilliance, and take effective action.

When receiving life coaching, you will likely experience problems with your coach. No matter whom you hire as a coach and how skilled that person is, your coach is going to make mistakes. When you talk theoretically about the mistakes coaches can make, you learn something useful. But when you're on the receiving end of those mistakes while you're paying for the service, you quickly become even more committed to avoiding those mistakes with your own clients.

The flip side of this benefit is that when you receive coaching, you also discover what's most empowering to you. I learned many of the most effective ways to be a life coach by receiving coaching from about a dozen people over the last 25 years.

One more benefit of receiving coaching is worth stating many times: When you use coaching to create a wonderful life, you bring that life to every interaction with your clients. You are doing what you ask clients to do—living the life of your dreams. And when clients perceive that, they can trust you even more.

Chapter Seven
Marketing Your Services

Three approaches to marketing

Life coaching can be an amazingly simple service to market. As you discover ways to build your client base, experiment with three basic tools: clarity, communication, and media.

Clarity

Marketing begins in the domain of being. Before you do anything else to promote yourself as a life coach, *be clear about the value that this service creates*. If you know from the depths of your soul that life coaching delivers tremendous benefits to people, then marketing can become a natural and spontaneous activity.

When approaching people about becoming my clients, my goal is not to "sell" life coaching. My aim is not to convince other people to buy this service. My goal is simply to explain life coaching fully and then assist others to see whether it's a service that would benefit them.

This is exactly how College Survival, Inc., used to market *Becoming a Master Student*, which became the best-selling college textbook in America. There could be a million explanations for that book's success, but I think a major reason is that we didn't sell the book in any traditional sense. We never tried to convince our customers that the book was a good buy for them. What we did say was, "Here's the book, and here's what it will provide for students. Is this something that would be useful for you?" We always had our eye on serving people, not selling the product.

You can adopt a similar approach to marketing life coaching. From the start, you can release any concern about whether or not a person buys the service. Instead, focus on assisting that person to have a more wonderful life. In the first few conversations you have with a potential client, you can just describe life coaching and explore how you could be of service. In effect, you say, "If life coaching sounds like something that you want, then I will be happy to sell my services to you. If this does not sound valuable, then I wouldn't even dream of wanting you to part with your time and money."

That spirit of service can continue even after people sign up for life coaching. Let's say you've been working with someone for a few months and you get signals that the coaching is not working for her. Rather than convince this person to remain as your client, look together to see if you can make the coaching more effective. Also assist her to see whether the coaching is creating value. If not, explore the option of ending the life coaching relationship.

Start marketing from your heart and soul—from your clarity about the value of coaching. This clarity comes before marketing strategies such as mailing brochures or placing advertisements. Strategies can be useful, but if you try to use them in the absence of clarity, the strategies usually fall flat. Instead, start from a premise (a stand, a commitment): *The service I offer is extremeluy valuable.* Add whatever strategies you want to this level of clarity, and you can succeed at marketing.

Communication

A second tool for marketing life coaching takes place in the domain of doing. And what I'm suggesting you do is communicate constantly. *Tell everyone you know about your service.* This is a personal service with a small client base. You'll probably be working with a dozen people or so, not thousands of customers. Even in the age of mass media, word of mouth is still the most effective way to market this kind of small business.

When you talk to people, focus on the benefits of life coaching. Many new life coaches don't do this. They often say something like,

"As your life coach, I'll get together with you once a week or so to help you define problems, brainstorm solutions, set goals, and move into action." That statement is about the *features* of life coaching.

Instead, I suggest that you speak about the *benefits* of life coaching—how people change while working with you. Talk about the results that your clients experience from life coaching. Describe how life coaching helps them create more health, happiness, wealth, and love in their lives. You could even provide an experience of coaching to a potential client by assisting them to set a goal or generate options for solving a problem.

My father was a salesman, and he was the first person to help me understand the difference between features and benefits. He used to say, "When people go into a hardware store, they aren't interested in buying a drill bit. They're trying to buy a hole." It took me years to figure out what he was talking about. What he meant was that *people want the benefit, not the feature*—in this case, the hole, not the drill bit. That's a distinction I want to keep in mind when speaking to potential life coaching clients.

This approach can become the marketing of the new millennium. In this kind of marketing, we focus on our purpose and on our service. There is no hype and no manipulation. We keep talking about the results and benefits of life coaching. There are no sales gimmicks, but there are lots of new customers.

Media

Your marketing efforts can also exist in the domain of having. When approaching potential clients, you can have plenty of promotional materials on hand—business cards, stationery, brochures with testimonials from your previous clients, videos, refrigerator magnets, monogrammed pens, calendars, post cards, and more. You could rent a billboard, put up a sign, or place an ad in the newspaper. You could even wear an "Ask me about life coaching" button and see how people respond.

179

Any of these materials could be useful. Besides promoting your service, they can educate people about life coaching. However, lack of materials can become an excuse to avoid talking about what you do ("I can't tell anyone about life coaching until I get my business cards printed and my video produced"). *If you gain clarity about the value of life coaching and skill in communicating about your service, you could find that your business flourishes even when you have no marketing materials at all.*

Some of the most effective and successful life coaches I know have no materials whatsoever—not even business cards.

Leaving a verbal calling card

There's great power in the practice of describing your life coaching service. Part of that power is that you can gain new clients. Equally important is being able to hear yourself speak about what you do as a life coach, and about who you are committed to being when you are with clients.

Potential clients often drift away for a few moments when they are told about life coaching as they start to imagine what having a life coach would be like. It can be so satisfying for them to think about having such a partner in their lives that they come back to the present moment looking refreshed. In a sense, they get to have a life coach for a few seconds, even if it's only in their imagination.

To market your service, I suggest that you practice leaving a "verbal calling card." Learn to describe life coaching in one minute or less. You can speak about your profession so clearly, so succinctly, and so powerfully that people will want to sign up as soon as you're done talking. In a relatively brief conversation, you can open up people to the possibility that life could be 10 times more wonderful than it is right now.

One way to create your own calling card is to borrow someone else's first. When learning to speak in a way that you've never spoken before, you can start by repeating someone else's words. This process is a little like the way a jazz musician learns to improvise. Only after mastering the basics of scales, chords, and arpeggios does she invent her own creative compositions.

The following example offers one version of the "perfect" calling card. Now, please keep that word *perfect* in quotation marks. These words, of course, are not perfect. They're probably different than the words you'll eventually use for your own calling card. Even so, this calling card offers a basic model you can use in speaking briefly and effectively about life coaching.

I recommend that you memorize this calling card and speak it a few times in the presence of other people:

> "My profession is life coaching. This is a long-term partnership where I help people create the life of their dreams. I promise that if we work together, your effectiveness will improve dramatically and you will experience even a more wonderful life than you do now.

> "I charge for this service by a monthly retainer. Clients pay me a thousand dollars a month up front for between six to eight hours of coaching each month. We communicate face-to-face, over the phone, and in writing.

> "In addition to money, there's something that's just as important to me—that you get great value from this coaching. I only want to be your life coach if you are making wonderful use of our time together and experiencing powerful and positive new results in your life. I do this work to make a living and to make a difference."

Once you have memorized that calling card, you can take elements of this example and develop your own calling card—or create something that's completely original. The following suggestions can help:

- *Put your calling card in writing.* Get together with other people to draft your cards, compare notes, and incorporate each other's ideas.

- *Rehearse.* Speak your calling card out loud, even if it's just to an empty chair. Pretend that a potential client is sitting across from you and that you are about to do your most powerful speaking about life coaching. The full benefit of a calling card lies not in writing it or memorizing it but in *speaking* it.

- *Be specific.* Offer a few important details about the benefits of life coaching. Avoid jargon and talk in terms that most people will immediately understand.

- *Explain what you don't do.* For example, explain how life coaching differs from consulting or counseling.

- *As you gain skill, re-invent your calling card each time you speak it.* People can recognize a canned pitch. Speak authentically in the moment and avoid reciting a memorized script.

- *After delivering your calling card and answering any questions about life coaching, consider going for a close.* Ask people if they'd like to meet with you to learn more, or if they'd like to set a date to start life coaching. Offer to begin working with people, and accept a "no" graciously and easily. Don't take the conversation further unless you get a firm yes. Trust that when people really want to work with you, they will come back.

Attracting clients you love to coach

Let clients self-select

Some new life coaches screen potential clients up front. They make assumptions about who might want a life coach and can afford it and who might not.

The problem with this approach is that for people who would love to have a life coach, it robs them of the opportunity to sign up. When first marketing your service, you'll probably have plenty of room for clients. So, I suggest that you invite everyone you know and let people self-select.

You never know when you're going to meet someone who wants life coaching as much as I want it. As I mentioned earlier, I would hire a life coach long before I bought a home or a second car. There are other people out there who will want life coaching that much once they discover what the service is about.

Consider many types of clients

I know a life coach in the Bay Area of California named Jerry Joiner. He is an accomplished and skillful person, originally trained as an obstetrician. Last time I talked to him he had over 25 coaching clients, and he told me that he keeps turning people away because he's too busy.

Before Jerry had any clients, he developed a list of the types of people he wanted to coach. For example, he wanted to work with a person who was dying, a person who was gay, a person who was poor, and someone who was a CEO for a major corporation.

You might find this approach useful. Many new life coaches possess a rather narrow vision of the kind of clients they could potentially have. Consider making a list of the people you'd probably never coach. Then contact at least one person on that list and describe your service.

Approach people with big goals

I like to work with people who have large-scale, long-term goals. These don't have to be philanthropic or humanitarian goals. It's okay with me if the goals are selfish as long as they are big.

This brings up another distinction between life coaching and counseling. People often go into a counseling relationship with relatively limited goals—for example, to grieve a parent's death, solve a marital problem, or learn to get along better with their children.

Those are all great goals, but I prefer to coach people with a larger vision. I enjoy a client who wants to take on his entire life and experience massive transformation. I like clients who already have a good life and want to have a phenomenal life.

People with large goals are often ideal candidates for life coaching. Chances are that they already have an expanded sense of possibility and a passion for personal development. What's more, their goals could take a long time to achieve, so they're more likely to enter into a long-term life coaching relationship. As you draw up your list of potential clients, consider people who already think big.

Approach older adults

When picturing typical candidates for life coaching, we could easily see in our mind's eye a group of people from around age 20 to age 50. I think it's great to add older people to our prospect list.

One thing I like about coaching older people is that they often have two important resources—discretionary time and money. By the time people turn 70 or 80, they're probably no longer working for a living or saving money to put children through school. They may have stopped thinking about how to manage their money or their time. As life coaches, we can bring older adults back to a conversation of the future. We can coach them about the use of leisure time, volunteer opportunities, and relationships with grandchildren. We can help them speak candidly with the people that they've loved and the people that they've hurt. We can listen until they've shared their wisdom and told their stories. We can assist these people to communicate fully so that they can age gracefully and die peacefully.

State your qualifications

Some people will want to know what qualifies you to be a life coach. You have many options for answering that question:

- *Speak about your training.* Even though you may not have had formal training in life coaching, you may have had training in teaching, counseling, or another helping profession. That training is relevant to your work as a life coach.

- *Talk about your experience.* You can talk about the clients you've had and the results they've generated through life coaching. If you've worked both as a life coach and a consultant or counselor, then you can talk from first-hand experience about how these fields differ.

- *Speak about your enthusiasm for personal growth.* Even if you don't have much experience as a life coach, you can still share your passion for personal and professional development. Since I was about 13 years old, my passion has been discovering success strategies and ways to communicate them. I took on this task wholeheartedly, first as a hobby and then as a profession. As a life coach, I trust that you share in this passion, and this is one of the key qualifications you bring to life coaching.

- *Describe the wonderful life you have.* Talk about the goals you've set and met. Reveal some the problems you've faced and the strategies you used to solve them. Also, speak candidly about your failures. When we know ways to learn from them, our mistakes can become our most patient and profound mentors. By celebrating mistakes, we can transform them into qualifications for life coaching.

- *Talk about processes that go beyond content.* Describe general strategies that clients can use to solve any problem, change any habit, and meet any goal.

- *Speak about your number one qualification—your commitment to serve.* Promise clients that you will keep each of them in your consciousness and root for them as much or even more than their parents or spouses do. Tell clients that you will hold their goals as sacred creations and assist them in any way you can to create the life of their dreams.

Meet other life coaches and recommend each other

People who run a one-person or home-based business can quickly become isolated. To market your service effectively, get to know other self-employed people. Especially seek out other life coaches. They might be willing to refer potential clients to you.

Offer your service to organizations

Another option is to approach employers and ask them to fund life coaching for their employees. Present life coaching as a benefit on a par with health insurance or long-term disability benefits. Talk about the potential gains to the company as clients gain more skill in managing time, creating long-term goals, and resolving conflict. When you discuss fees, consider offering a "bulk discount" if the company delivers you a certain number of clients.

Be prepared to answer objections and questions

Following in italics are some of the comments you may hear when you first describe life coaching to people—along with some possible ways for you to respond.

"Coaching sounds pretty unusual."
"Yes, life coaching is an unusual profession. Whenever you're ready, I'd like to explain it in more detail and talk about the potential benefits that life coaching has for you."

"Why do you want to coach me?"
"Because I see you as an effective and contributing person who wants to have the most wonderful life you can imagine. Also, I'm looking for new clients, and I'd love to work with you."

"I don't want to do life coaching for years."
"When you work with me, you're not committed to use my service for years. I just want to hold out the option of a long-term relationship. You can pay me by the month and cancel at any time."

"I don't need a life coach. I'm getting all the benefits of life coaching through my close friends. We take turns helping each other, and it doesn't cost any money. Why should I hire you?"
"Congratulations. That's wonderful. I'm really pleased for you. And if it ever turns out that you're not getting those benefits through your close friends, then give me a call.

"Sometimes I can provide what friends can't. I find that even my best friends can have an agenda for me, so it's hard for them to help me look in an unbiased way at what I want. I also have experience in working with many people to set and achieve their goals, solve problems, and change habits. That experience is something that many friends can't offer you.

"If you like, I could be with you for two or three hours at no charge as a way to demonstrate the benefits of life coaching. It would be useful for me to know if your friends are actually providing these benefits."

"Everything in my life is great."
"Wonderful. Not everyone can say that they're living the life of their dreams. If you ever want something else—more money, health, vitality, or more spark in your marriage—then call me.

"I also want to hold out the option that your life could be even more tremendous than it is right now. We might be able to invent some possibilities you've never considered, such as living a life with no money worries at all, or learning how to have a one-hour orgasm.

"And if your life is already full and satisfying, then we could look at some new ways for you to contribute to others. There's certainly no shortage of problems to tackle—everything from ending hunger to preventing teen suicide. Given that you have such a wonderful life, you could take on a big problem and make a world-class contribution."

Making the transition to self-employment

Many people who start life coaching go from a structured corporate setting to a fully self-generated business, probably working at home. This can be a huge transition, going from 45 to 50 hours at work each week to perhaps 10 or 15 hours of life coaching. If becoming a life coach involves this kind of career change for you, then consider some strategies for making a smooth transition to self-employment.

Set goals

You can begin by practicing a skill we recommend to clients—setting and meeting goals. Planning assists you to move from an environment where others structure your time to an environment where you do all the structuring.

As you plan your new career, you can set many kinds of goals. To begin, consider when you'd like to start seeing clients, the number and types of clients you want to work with, and the amount of income you want to generate. After brainstorming some ideas, list the specific outcomes you want to achieve in each area and write a specific action plan for achieving them. Set due dates for each outcome where appropriate.

When you set goals, you become the "author" of your future. I suggest that you create like authors do and put your plan in writing. The act of writing lends clarity and substance to your plan.

Make the change gradually

I made the transition to self-employment gradually. I went to my boss and told him that I was starting a company and I wanted to cut back from working more than full-time to working a regular 40-hour week. He said yes, so then I put in my overtime hours at my new business. Later, I went back to him and asked if I could work two-thirds time so that I could work the other third plus overtime at my new business. I continued cutting back at my job, going from half-time to quarter-time and finally to "no-time." The whole transition took about 18 months.

This is not necessarily the "right" way to make the transition to self-employment, but it certainly is an option for you to consider.

Find partners

Another way to structure your home-based business is to recruit some partners. For example, you might find somebody who could help you get organized, such as office assistant or secretary. This person would not have to work with you full-time. Consider someone who has a secretarial business at home and is willing to work with you periodically.

When I first started my business, I wanted a secretary and in no way could afford one. So I found a woman who provided support services to many small businesses. I dictated letters and mailed her the tapes. She typed my correspondence and sent it back to me for editing. She also came to my office periodically to help me organize my desk. Getting this kind of support is one way to promote a successful home business.

Another option is to hire someone to coach you in developing your business. To build the most empowering relationship with this person, explain the difference between coaching and consulting and indicate which type of relationship you want at any given time. Teach this person how to coach you.

Set aside working hours

When I started my own business, I loved the flexibility of setting my work schedule. I could go to a movie during the middle of the day, if I wanted, or go outside and take a walk. In addition to preserving that kind of flexibility, I also wanted to set a consistent schedule so that my body would know when it was time to start working. So, I set aside blocks of time for work. At one point, for example, my plan was to put in four hours of work between 6 a.m. and noon. Then take a two-hour lunch break and work another four hours between 2 p.m. and 6 p.m.

Now, of course, I deviated from that schedule occasionally when something fun came up during the day or in emergency situations. At the same time, this flexible schedule was enough to signal my psyche and my body when it was time for work and time to relax.

This is the same strategy used by people who go to church regularly at the same time each week. When that time approaches, their whole spirit enters a sacred space. Employers who ask you to show up from 8 a.m. to 5 p.m. Monday through Friday are also creating a space for you to do your most productive work.

By the way, I am not recommending that you work 8 to 5. I am suggesting that you set aside a work schedule that's both consistent and flexible. Also schedule work hours around your personal patterns—the times of the day when you feel most alert and productive. Creating that kind of space in time sets you up to do your most effective work.

One more suggestion: Start slowly and schedule in a lot of down time. Consider starting with 15 or 20 hours a week for direct client contact. You'll need other time to clear yourself between clients, find new clients, and pursue your own professional development. Focus on producing results with your clients, not on working a certain number of hours. Through life coaching, I believe that you can contribute dramatically to people in a short amount of time.

Set aside a physical space

In addition to setting aside your work hours—your "time space"—consider setting aside a physical space for life coaching. When arriving in that space, your mind and body will know that it's time to work. Your subconscious mind can associate that room with full contribution through life coaching. If possible, set up your work space so that you only do work in that space.

Perhaps you don't have enough room for a separate office. No problem. Your space for life coaching could be a corner of a room. It could also be any spot where you can place appropriate symbols—flowers, a particular clock, a mounted photograph, or any other object with a special meaning for you that's connected with effective life coaching.

Set aside certain clothes

You can experiment with adopting a "costume" for work. One of the advantages of working at home, particularly if you spend a lot of time on the phone, is that you don't have to get dressed up. Even so, you might want to set aside clothes to wear only when you work—say, a certain pair of shoes or certain clothes. Doing so sends yourself a message: *These are the shoes I wear when I am working, and I don't wear these shoes when I am off work.* Then your clothes become another way to signal yourself that you've entered a space for contributing to the world through life coaching.

Set your fees

Fees for life coaching vary widely. Life coaching clients could pay anywhere from nothing to hundreds of dollars per hour or thousands of dollars per month. When choosing what to charge for your services, you've got plenty of room for creativity.

One option is to charge by the hour. You could also charge by the month and offer a range of hours that clients can be in contact with you. For example: "My fee for life coaching is $500 per month. For that, you get between four and eight hours of time with me during the month, either in person or over the phone."

Or, charge a flat fee with no time limit. I know a life coach who charges $2,000 per month. For that price, his clients can have as much coaching time as they want. What he discovered is that most people only want a few hours per week.

Monthly fees have some advantages over hourly fees. When you charge by the hour, clients may keep their eyes on the clock. Charging by the month minimizes that outcome. I don't want clients to focus on how many hours they're getting with me. I want them to focus on results—the wonderful life they intend to create.

What's more, monthly fees promote long-term relationships with clients. Life coaching is not a quick fix (or any kind of fix at all). This is a long-term, committed partnership—much more like a marriage than a date.

Another life coach I know charges $18,000 per year per client. He asks clients to pay that fee in monthly installments, but he refers to it as a yearly retainer. (This man generally works with people who make over $200,000 a year, and many of them spend about $18,000 per year on car payments or travel so they don't complain about spending this much for the life of their dreams.) Working with clients on a yearly basis keeps them focused on producing long-term results—and helps secure your transition to self-employment.

For years, I've provided coaching for no charge. I did this as my contribution to leaders of nonprofit organizations. Four years ago, I started to charge for my coaching. I charged $10,000 a year to my first client, but that just didn't seem like enough. The second and third clients I charged paid me $100,000 a year, and that is now my standard fee, except I still provide some people a year of life coaching for no charge. The point is, flexibility is one key when you set your fees.

Chapter Eight
Questions and Answers About Life Coaching

The following questions represent just the tip of the iceberg of what coaching students have asked me over the last many years. Like any good question, I believe that the inquiry is more important than the answer. I present these questions more for their value as questions than for the value of the answers. The purpose of my answer is to spark your creativity and open up the inquiry, not to provide "the answer."

As you continue your professional development, please formulate many questions and then create multiple answers for each of them.

I am interested in your questions. Please send them to me at Dave@FallingAwake.com or mail them to my address listed in the front of this book.

Questions about life coaching as a career

Is life coaching an elitist field?

Life coaching is usually a high-end service for wealthier people, like the service provided by a lawyer or even a massage therapist. This is not surprising. In our society, people with more money generally get more services.

It's also possible that a single parent with three jobs might need life coaching, and that she could pay something for it. Maybe the leader of your favorite nonprofit organization wants a life coach, but the organization has a tight budget. In either of these cases, you could be the coach. It just depends on how you structure your fees. For clients with less money, you could do pro-bono work like lawyers.

Or, you could charge these clients just a little, say $5 per hour. Or, you could ask for funding from a foundation to work with such clients.

In 1987, I started The Brande Foundation and its current primary project is to provide life coaching at no charge. Through the foundation, we provide one to three years of life coaching to leaders of national and international foundations with annual budgets in excess of $5 million. You can find out more about this program at www.BrandeFoundation.org.

Could I coach someone who has other life coaches?

Absolutely. I take care of myself so well that I have four part-time professional life coaches, and they, in effect, work as a team.

As a client, I could also imagine making an appointment with an agency that has several life coaches on staff. This agency could have a file on me. When I make an appointment, I'd receive no guarantees about which person I'd see, except that it would be a highly skilled coach. I think this kind of arrangement could work well, and there are precedents for it in other professions, such as health care.

This agency would hire life coaches who were available a certain number of hours each week, and the agency would manage appointments, billing, and marketing. I currently know of no place like that for life coaches, but I love the idea. So, go for it!

Do I need to know people before approaching them as potential clients?

You can develop a trusting relationship with a new person in five minutes. Massage therapists do. You can be with somebody in such a way that they will immediately want to know more about life coaching. This might be the person sitting next to you on the plane or some other complete stranger. On the other hand, you might have five or ten conversations with people before they sign up. It just depends on the circumstances and the person.

A friend of mine just signed up a client at the barbershop. He was getting his hair cut and overheard a doctor sitting next to him complaining about his marriage. After a short conversation, a new life coaching relationship was started.

Questions about coaching people who seem "stuck"

How can I respond when clients keep canceling sessions, even though they say that they want to continue?

I like to believe people by their words and not their actions. I know that this is contrary to how many people operate. I believe my client's words. And the words from the client in this question are that he wants to continue. I suggest that you believe that and keep acting consistently with it.

Instead of interpreting his canceling as not wanting to continue, you can choose a more powerful interpretation for this fact: "He's completely overwhelmed." "He's way too busy." "He's having a trauma in his life that really calls for my assistance." Those are just a few possibilities.

If you hold such an interpretation, your actions will be much different than they would be if you assumed he didn't want coaching. In fact, you may even step up your outreach. You could call him every single day, maybe twice a day. You could write him letters or send him a post card every day: "Dear John, I know you want to continue meeting with me. You acknowledged how much value there is in life coaching and said you want to be in touch with me. Please call."

Then you could stop in at his office. Like an effective salesperson, you go in to the prospect's office and wait, knowing that if you wait long enough, your client will come out and talk to you. You just drive over there and *know* that he wants to talk to you. How do you know that? Because he said so.

195

Eventually, he will either talk to you or change the way he speaks about life coaching. If he no longer wants to continue, believe him and stop your outreach.

How can I help clients move beyond resignation?

Hopelessness and resignation show up in many different ways as clients speak: "That's just not possible for me." "I could never get that done." "There's no hope that I'll ever lose weight. I've tried every diet. I've just got bad hormones."

Whenever you hear a client's resignation, you've got several options:

- *Model the sense of possibility.* Be clear that there's hope. Don't buy into their helplessness and don't bond with people on the basis of their wounds. Recall your commitment to see each client as brilliant, loving, and creative. When you do that consistently, it's hard for clients to stay resigned.
- *Let people immerse themselves in resignation.* Let them fully experience hopelessness and even wallow in it. Assist them to wallow in a useful way, though—to completely express the upset, hurt, and pain. Any emotion that's completely experienced will eventually disappear.
- *Help your clients generate lots of options.* You can even acknowledge your client's resignation while you help them generate options by saying something like: "I know it doesn't look like you have many options right now, but are you open to some ideas?" Then encourage clients to invent at least 10 possibilities. When they're done, you can invent 10 more. That can be enough to shift people out of hopelessness.
- *Shift the conversation* to some other behavior or circumstance that the client can change.
- *Set up a role play:* "If a friend of yours was feeling as resigned as you feel right now, what would you say to her?
- *Remind clients of ways in which they are powerful and effective:* "Let's leave this topic for a moment. Tell me about an area where you've had some success recently."

- *Stop talking and do something physical.* Take a walk with the client. Do some t'ai chi or yoga. Movement can trigger a shift in thinking and feeling as much as—or even more—than anything you say.

- *Treat the resignation as if it is nothing more than a habit.* Suggest that whenever the client notices he is repeating this habit, he can gently let it go and replace it with another set of behaviors by: committing to change the habit, setting up a feedback system, and practicing without reproach.

How can I assist clients to choose from a variety of options?

This is a problem I encounter often: Clients succeed at generating a long list of options, and then they find it hard to choose one option to implement.

When this happens, I affirm and allow client's confusion. Then I ask them to just pick one option for now—any option. After "trying on" this option for a few minutes, clients might say, "No, I really don't think this is the one I want."

"Great," I reply. "Now we've eliminated one option and pared down the list."

At that point, I ask clients to choose another option, and we repeat the process until they select one of the options that they can experiment with for a while. The essential strategy here is to let clients sit with each option for a few minutes until they arrive at one that feels on track for them.

Questions about staying effective as a life coach

Who am I to be a life coach, anyway?

You don't have to be perfect in order to be a life coach. You could even assist people to be more effective than you are yourself. When you do, you're like the coaches who work with Olympic athletes—coaches who have never been Olympic athletes themselves.

As a coach, you can take people to places you've not been—to levels of skill beyond your own. The value you provide is not necessarily in teaching skills but in letting clients know you completely stand for their success and in providing an opportunity for them to realize their full potential and their dreams.

How can I coach people when my own life's not working that well?

You can coach people about money even if you've got a stack of unpaid bills. You can coach people about their relationships even if your own marriage is in crisis. And, you can assist people to achieve vibrant health even when you're low on energy.

Some of your clients may not believe this at first. They might ask: "How can you coach me when you can't even manage your own life?"

That's a tough question, and here is one possible way to answer: "I'm glad you brought that up. You know a lot of times people think this and they won't say it. Thanks for speaking so candidly.

"I think I can be of great assistance to you, and all the stuff that's going on in my life right now actually empowers me to do that. I would prefer to have a life coach who has some major problems in her own life. So far I haven't met anybody who can honestly say they have not experienced major problems in life.

"Also, I've made great progress. First of all, I know my relationships are not working as well as they could. And I know that my financial life is not working as well as it could. But I've made major advances in these areas, and I've learned a lot. In fact, I'm now more qualified to help others in these areas than I was before... because of what I have learned from all of my mistakes.

"What's more, I think it's much easier to assist other people than it is to assist myself. My job as a life coach is not to give you advice, and it's not to tell you how I solved my problems. My role is to help you generate your own solutions and uncap your own brilliance. And I do that first of all by asking you to define what you want in every area of your life and then create ways to get it."

Is it useful for me to meet with a client's relatives, coworkers, or friends?

Yes. Meeting with people who know your client allows you to go beyond the limits of an exclusively one-to-one relationship with that person. I realize that this has the potential of violating the ethics of a confidential relationship—but it can work well depending on how you set up the meetings with the other people.

My friend and skilled life coach, Richard Kiefer told me about a client of his with a serious illness. He met with one of this client's relatives at the client's request, and that meeting helped the relative accept the reality of the illness. In his work with leaders of non-profit organizations, Stan Lankowitz has also met with the client's staff members.

Is it ever useful to behave outrageously on purpose to get a point across during a coaching session?

No. Now, there are some counselors who use this technique and call it provocative therapy. For example, if they have a client who is very passive, then one of these therapists might just sit there and talk about his life for an entire hour and wait for the client to get mad and interrupt. Or, when working with an obese client, a provocative therapist might begin a session by saying, "Man, are you ever fat!" trusting that this comment will shock the client into taking responsibility for his weight.

These are pretty outrageous examples, and as a life coach I would not do these things. My goal is to be as honest and authentic as possible and not to behave with a hidden purpose.

How do I stay grounded in process and avoid getting lost in the content of a client's problems?

You can start by simply committing to stay with the process; then just keep practicing. For example, I practice when I watch the news on television. Instead of focusing on the content of a news story— the *who, what, when, where* and *why*—I stick with the *how*, the way that the content is delivered. I'll ask who the president is being right now. He might be talking about creating peace in the Middle East, but is he *being* peaceful?

You can do the same at any meeting. If you find the content boring, just shift your attention to how skilled the people are at the processes of effective speaking and listening.

I once heard the director of the Boston Philharmonic talk about directing an orchestra. I didn't find the content of his speech to be very interesting, but I was fascinated with who he was being—so enthusiastic, so involved, so loving and focused and committed to his art.

Another way you can stay grounded in process is to talk about specific processes with your clients. I sometimes do this with the 23 Power Processes and the 12 Success Strategies described in Chapter Five. You could even focus on one process per week with a client and talk about all the ways that each process could help clients get what they want. This approach gives you the basis for almost six months of life coaching with a built-in advertisement of what's to come each week that you meet.

My initial meeting with a client was so powerful that I'm afraid I can't live up to that first session. How do I get past this fear?

When you produce great results in any area—no matter whether it's in coaching or art or athletics—you sometimes get stage fright. That's natural.

One thing you can do is acknowledge the fear right up front to the client: "You know, I am still amazed at how powerful our last session was, and I'm not sure that it can ever happen again in that way."

A second option is to not take that first session personally. When clients move dramatic distances in a short time, that's probably due to the client—not to you. So, if your first session is powerful, you can congratulate the client and hold out for even greater possibilities: "You were brilliant the last time we met, and I know you can be even more brilliant." Keep acknowledging that the power of the life coaching relationship comes from your client.

Bring your own questions and answers

One purpose of any chapter full of questions and answers is to share some specific ideas in an interesting and direct format. In presenting these questions and answers about life coaching, I also have another purpose—to help you pose your own questions about life coaching.

Throughout this book, I've noted the possible dangers in asking questions when coaching. However, in a teaching environment, questions can create value in several ways:

- When you ask a question, you bring a huge gift to people—an invitation for them to speak their brilliance and an offer to listen to their answers. Full listening is one of the best ways that we can contribute to others, especially in a culture that doesn't particularly value listening . . . or at least doesn't practice it.
- Questions open up an inquiry that might never have taken place. Questions wake people up and lead them to examine an issue that might go unexamined. Questions can take conversations into new areas, lead to new information, promote curiosity, create new distinctions, and multiply possibilities.
- Questions remind us that no one knows everything about any subject. Through questions, we can go beyond the knowledge of any individual and access the knowledge of an entire group of people.

In addition to experiencing these general benefits, you can ask questions leading to answers that will dramatically improve your ability to coach people. Following are some ways to discover such questions for yourself.

Write something you're sure of and put a question mark after it

Perhaps one of the things you know about life coaching is that you never give advice. In that case, you could write, *I don't give advice to people?* That suggests another question: *Is there ever a circumstance when I could serve people most by giving them advice?* Powerful questions sometimes take tried and true "facts" and lead us to doubt them. And that can be a valuable stimulus to learn, grow, and improve.

Ask about what's missing

Another way to invent a useful question is to notice what's missing from your life coaching practice and then ask a question about how to supply it. For example, if you want more clients, you can write, *What's missing for me is skill in marketing. How can I get more clients?* Or, *What's missing is time. What are some ways that I could create time in my day to actually do the coaching that I say I want to do?*

A related strategy is to take something that's present in your life and ask how to be free of it. So if you find yourself distracted whenever you meet with a certain client, you could ask, *What are some ways that can I stay focused and be free of distractions when meeting with clients?*

Just let your pen start moving

Sometimes you can access a deeper level of knowing by just taking out your pen, putting it on a piece of paper and starting to write—even before you know what to write. Don't think. Just watch your fingers and see *what* they write. The results might be surprising.

You can do the same thing by speaking. Just open your mouth and say, "The question I most want to ask is…" Then, listen to what comes out of your mouth before you start thinking about how to complete the sentence.

Pretend to be someone else

Another way to invent questions is to first think of someone that you greatly respect. Then pretend you're that person and ask the question you think she would ask.

You could also think of a person you admire and imagine what question you'd ask this person. Imagine that you're face-to-face with Jesus, Buddha, the Dalai Lama, or whomever else you choose and this person says, "My friend, I grant you one question. I'll answer anything. Now, what do you most want to know?"

Ask what else you want to know

Many times you can quickly generate questions by simply asking, "What else do I want to know about this?" You can do this right after you read a paragraph in a book or listen to someone speak.

For example, in Chapter Five I write about how to prioritize goals by assigning them letters (the "ABC priority system"). After reading those paragraphs, you might think of several other things you'd like to know, such as:

- What's the value of setting priorities in the first place?
- What happens if I don't set a priority for a goal? Could that sometimes be effective?
- How else can I represent priorities besides using letters?

Begin a general question, then brainstorm endings

Beginning a general question and brainstorming a long list of endings can help you invent a question that you've never asked before. For instance:

- *What do I do when...?* What do I do when a client's attracted to me? What do I do when clients don't pay? What do I do when clients don't show up on time? What do I do when I get too many clients? What do I do when I don't have any clients?

- *How can I...?* How can I get just the kind of clients I want? How can I expand my client base? How can I double my income? How can I take a month-long vacation when I want to be in touch with my clients every week? How can I become a more effective life coach?

- *When do I...?* When do I call it quits with a client? When do I meet with clients in person rather than over the phone? When do I touch clients?

One final note: You might not be satisfied with some of the answers I give in this chapter or even many of the questions I raise. If that's true, then remember that, like your clients, you are brilliant. You are creative. And you are a genius. Every sentence in this chapter and in this book is an invitation for you to invent your own questions—and, more importantly, your own answers. This is one of the most powerful ways I know to promote your ongoing development as a life coach.

Bibliography

Bolles, Richard N. *The Three Boxes of Life and How to Get Out of Them: An Introduction to Life/Work Planning*, Berkeley, CA: Ten Speed Press, 1978.

Covey, Stephen R, A. Roger Merrill, and Rebecca Merrill. *First Things First*, New York: Simon & Schuster, 1994.

Dominguez, Joe and Vicki Robin. *Your Money or Your Life: Transforming Your Relationship with Money and Achieving Financial Independence*, New York: Viking, 1992.

Ellis, Dave. *Becoming a Master Student*, Boston: Houghton Mifflin, 1981 rev. 2003 (10th edition).

Ellis, Dave. *Creating Your Future: Five Steps to the Life of Your Dreams*, Boston: Houghton Mifflin, 1998.

Ellis, Dave. *Falling Awake: Creating the Life of your Dreams*, Rapid City, SD: Breakthrough Enterprises, 2002.

Ellis, Dave and Stan Lankowitz. *Human Being: A Manual for Happiness, Health, Love, and Wealth*, Rapid City, SD: Breakthrough Enterprises, 1995.

Ellis, Dave, Stan Lankowitz, Ed Stupka, and Doug Toft. *Career Planning*, Boston: Houghton Mifflin, 1997.

Frankl, Viktor. *Man's Search for Meaning*, New York: Simon & Schuster, 1970.

Gawain, Shakti. *Creative Visualization*, Mill Valley, CA: Whatever Publishing, 1978.

Goldberg, Marilee C. *The Art of the Question: A Guide to Short-term Question-Centered Therapy*, New York: John Wiley & Sons, 1998.

Keyes, Ralph. *Timelock: How Life Got So Hectic and What You Can Do About It*, New York: HarperCollins, 1991.

Lakein, Alan. *How to Get Control of Your Time and Your Life*, New York: New American Library, 1974.

Reamer, Frederic G. *Tangled Relationships: Managing Boundary Issues in the Human Services*, New York: Columbia University Press, 2001.

Sher, Barbara with Annie Gottlieb. *Wishcraft: How To Get What You Really Want*, New York: Ballantine, 1979.

Sinetar, Marsha. *Do What You Love, The Money Will Follow*, New York: Dell, 1987.

Williams, Pat and Deborah C. Davis. *Therapist as Life Coach: Transforming Your Practice*, New York: W. W. Norton, 2002.

Williams, Pat and Lloyd J. Thomas. *Total Life Coaching: 50+ Life Lessons, Skills, and Techniques to Enhance your Practice AND your Life*, New York: W. W. Norton, 2005.

In addition, resources on life coaching are available from the following organization:

International Coach Federation, 2365 Harrodsburg Rd, Suite A325, Lexington, KY 40504. Tel: 888-423-3131, 859-219-3580. Fax: 888-329-2423, 859-226-441. www.coachfederation.org.

About the author

Over the last 25 years, Dave Ellis has helped over four million people create a more wonderful life through his workshops, books, and life coaching. He works primarily with already successful people who recognize that they could wake up every day experiencing abundant happiness, health, love, and wealth.

Dave is the author of seven books including *Becoming a Master Student*, which is the best-selling college textbook in America. His newest books are about life coaching and visioning and are titled, *Falling Awake* and *Life Coaching*.

He now facilitates workshops, teaches life coaches, and is president of The Brande Foundation. He has given away millions of dollars.

Dave practices what he teaches and is often described by his friends as the happiest person they know with an amazingly wonderful life. He is married and has four grown daughters.

Life coach training—a 15-month curriculum

The material in this book is the basis of a comprehensive 15-month training program to prepare people for a career in life coaching and for certification by the International Coach Federation. Development activities in this program include videotapes, intensive in-person workshops, teleconferences, individual life coaching, and one-on-one mentoring.

The first six months of the program focus on the personal development of the participant and includes individualized coaching experiences and personal/professional growth workshops. The next nine months focus on the development and supervised practice of specific coaching skills.

You can find out more about this training by visiting www.LifeCoachBook.com or by writing to:

Bill Rentz
PO Box 8396
Rapid City, SD 57709
USA

Index

ABC priority system   130, 203
acceptance   51, 154
  unconditional   7
acknowledgments   45
acquired traits   94
acting courageously (power
    process)   156
action plans   15, 16, 31, 38, 47, 54,
    81, 122
  double   134, 188
  multiple   66–7
active listening   54–5
addictions   143, 169
adding to client's list of
    possibilities (coaching
    continuum)   47, 57
  avoiding   56
advice   19, 48, 61-5
  breaking habit of giving   62
  case against   62
  giving   64
  giving, by sharing or
    questioning   47, 64
  responding to requests for   63
affirmations   60, 71, 135
affirming   49, 51, 70, 105–6, 161
African Americans   52
age   18, 184
agendas   17, 31
  conflicting   164
  for sessions   32–3, 42
  writing down   53
  see also sessions
agreement for life coaching   26,
    28, 169, 170, 173
alcoholics anonymous   19
altars   98

American Psychiatric Association
    27, 167
"and" versus "or"   123
anger   140
appreciating mistakes (power
    process)   155
appreciations   44–5
asking the client to generate a few
    possibilities (coaching
    continuum)   47
asking the client to generate many
    possibilities (coaching
    continuum)   47
assignments   41–2, 81, 82, 170
assisting versus insisting   100, 171
attachment versus preference   142
attention   37
  to attention   36–7
  drifting of   37, 38
  focused   7, 37, 155
audiotaping   80
authentic speaking   50, 85, 133,
    182
automatic behavior   150

Becoming a Master Student (Ellis)
    177
"be here now"   155
being   8
  focus on   72–3
  oriented   9
benefits of life coaching   4–10
benefits versus features   179
bigotry   51
blame   7, 103, 104, 146
blank canvas   17
boasting   91

body and listening   49
body language   81
boredom   70, 140, 141
bragging   91
brainstorming   39, 67, 107, 120,
     170, 188
   from questions   204
   passions and goals   74, 106
   solutions promoted by   134,
     135
breathing   53
   for emotional expression   142
brilliance, unlocking and
     uncovering   1–2, 48, 70, 108,
     176, 199
burnout   52
Burns, George   126

calendars   132, 138
candor   113, 120, 133, 134, 153,
     155, 156, 185
   asking for permission to employ
     160
cards (3×5)
   for distractions   37–8
   passions written on   74, 75
   in two-week planning   129
career of life coaching   3, 19–21
celebrations   2, 4, 31, 45, 54, 98,
     100
ceremonies   45, 98-9
change as benefit of life coaching
     8
chanting   98
"chat" sessions   25
check-ins   33
chemical dependency   169
children   70, 127
choosing your conversations and
     your community (power
     process)   155
Christian schools   126
churches   124
Civil Rights Movement   128
clarity in marketing   177–8

clearing   87
client-centered techniques   92
clients
   assignments for   41–2, 44, 82,
     170
   balancing intimacy with   90,
     159–60
   big goals of   183
   change in all domains and   8
   complaints and celebrations of
     31
   creating value from coaching
     119
   creativity of   5
   defensiveness in   102
   energy of   2
   exact words of   40
   failures of, to follow through
     100, 101
   feedback from   66, 76, 80, 81
   goals of   28, 183
   hopelessness in   196
   life survey of   20, 29
   notes and   32, 39–41
   obligations, limitations, and
     fears of   2
   permission from   80, 108, 119,
     160
   potential   178, 179, 180, 182,
     184, 185, 194
   referrals for   166–70
   resignation in   196–7
   self-selection of   182–3
   sexual attraction and   161
   speaking withheld information
     111–2
   strengths and special interests of
     132–4
   "stuck"   195–7
   successful nature of   2, 27
   types of   183
   values and commitments of   8,
     23
   visions of   4
   vulnerability of   90

see also life-coaching agreements;
    sessions
clinical depression   136
clinical psychologists   20
closure   45
clothes for work   190–1
coaching continuum, *see* life-
    coaching continuum
coaching preparation form   35
co-counseling   140
code of ethics   164
College Survival, Inc.   99, 144,
    166, 168, 177
commitments
    in changing habits   136
    of clients   8
    to clients   8, 10, 28
communication
    full   112
    in marketing   177
complaints   31, 75–6
compliments   152–3
confidentiality   2, 13, 27, 32, 117,
    141, 172, 173–4
conflicting agendas   164
conflicts of clients   30
confrontational approaches   7
consulting   19, 61, 114, 142
content versus process   102,
    153–4, 185, 200
continuing professional
    development   174–6
continuum, *see* life-coaching
    continuum
contributing (power process)   155
conversations
    balancing   126–7
    choosing   155, 156
    types of   84–9
cosmic consciousness   97
costs of life coaching, *see* fees for
    life coaching
counseling and life coaching   1,
    19, 164, 183
couples coaching   108–12

courage   133
*Creating Your Future: Five Steps to
    the Life of Your Dreams* (Ellis)
    29, 119, 122, 154
    see also future, creating
creativity
    as benefit of life coaching   5
    development of   95–8
crimes   27, 173–4
culture   52, 62, 137, 201
cycle of discovery, intention, action
    121

debriefing   53, 86–7
debt   6, 31
Declaration of Independence   172
defensiveness in clients   102
defining values, aligning actions
    (power process)   156
delegating   130
Denver, John   126
depression   139, 167
    clinical   136
    habitual   136
detaching and playing full out
    (power process)   155
determining what you want
    (power process)   154
diagnoses   103–4
*Diagnostic and Statistical Manual of
    Mental Disorders*   20, 27, 167
    see also mental disorders
directive techniques   47, 59, 92,
    108, 117
discovery, intention, action cycle
    121
discussion and debate   88
distraction   36–8, 74, 120, 155, 156
doing   8, 72
down time   175, 190
dreams, speaking   121–2
dual relationships   163–4

ecstasy   3
education, continuing   174–5

effectiveness coaches   166
effectiveness of life coaches   176,
    180, 197–201
ego equation   145
"either-or" mind set   123
elitist field   193–4
e-mail   23, 25, 42
embarrassment   111, 140–1
emotional discharge   76, 140–1,
    142
empathetic listening   48
    see also listening
employees and employers   161,
    163-5
empowering people   47, 60, 66,
    94, 118, 189
empty chair technique   112
energy renewal   52–3
enjoying and celebrating (power
    process)   155
ethics code   164
evaluations
    at College Survival, Inc.   99
    of life coaching   78-83
    self-   81-3
examining moment-to-moment
    choices (power process)
    154
exercise   53
expectations   117–8, 120, 155,
    156
external locus of control   61
eye contact   159

families   73–4
family history   94
faxes   23, 42
fears   2, 148
features versus benefits   179
feedback
    from clients   66, 76, 80, 81
    systems   138-9
feeding back
    celebrations, dreams, and
        actions   47, 54, 71

client's exact words   40
    dilemma   63
    passions and goals   70–1
    problem   97–8, 103, 142
fees for life coaching   25, 28, 186,
    191–2, 193–4
first session   28–31, 173
flexibility in sessions   23
focus in sessions   36–9, 79
focused attention   7, 37, 155
focusing attention (power process)
    155
follow up on assignments   42
formal assessments   30
free will versus God's will   126
Freudian psychoanalysis   94
friendship   1, 19, 111
fully listening, *see* listening, fully
fully listening and feeding back the
    problem (coaching
    continuum)   51, 53, 70
    with your answer   49
future
    creating   20, 71, 73, 95, 101,
        122–34 (*see also Creating Your
        Future: Five Steps to the Life of
        Your Dreams*)
    creative possibilities for   70
    helping client to move into
        46
    passions for   76
    predicting and worrying about
        127
    short-term and long-term   122
    visions for   16, 122
futurists   127

gay people   18
gender   18
genetic predispositions   94, 136,
    139
genius   1, 5, 11, 82, 106, 134, 140,
    154
giving advice, *see* advice
giving the answer   61

goals
    breaking of, into smaller steps
        107
    as commitments and holding
        lightly   101
    from complaints   75–6
    God's will and   125–6
    in life coaching   1, 27
    passions and   70–1, 74
    revising   124
    for self-employment   188
    setting of, versus spontaneity
        123–5
    specific   127
God   96, 97, 125–6
Grameen Bank   149
Great Spirit   97
group   25
guilt   6, 101

habit changing   7, 71, 136–40, 187,
    197
Handbook to Higher Consciousness
    (Keyes)   142
having, doing, and being   8
home-based businesses   185,
    188
hopelessness   196
hospice care   167
"how" versus "what"   126, 128
*Human Being: A Manual for
    Happiness, Health, Love, and
    Wealth* (Ellis, Lankowitz)   9,
    29, 119, 154

ignorance, benefits of   114–5
"I have a dream" speech (King)
    128
"I have to"   16, 106
illegal activities   171–2, 173
I-messages   60, 146–8
incense   98
income level   18, 143
insight   20
insisting versus assisting   100, 171

intentions   121
internal locus of control   61
internet   25
interpretations   14, 15, 16, 103–4,
    148
    managing   155
    versus observations   142, 147
interruptions   110, 120
intimacy   3, 77, 159–63
    balance of, with clients
        159–60
    secrets and   111–2
intuition   95–8
investigating role (power process)
    155
"I should"   16, 106

Jackins, Harvey   140
Jefferson, Thomas   172
jogging   24
Joiner, Jerry   24, 183
journaling   53, 87
judgments   6, 147
    release of   50–1, 103
    suspending   75

Keyes, Ken   142
Kiefer, Richard   199
King, Martin Luther   128

labeling   103, 146
language
    of obligation   106–7, 146
    of possibility   106
    of preference   106
Lankowitz, Stan   9, 29, 119, 143,
    199
laws, state   172
learning styles   24
legal protection   26
letters, coaching with   23, 24,
    42
    see also writing
licensed mental health
    professionals   27

life coaches
  breaking advice habit by
      62–3
  commitment of 5, 8, 10, 28, 30
  renewing 32
  effectiveness of 197–201
  energy renewal for 52–3
  enhancing skills of 69–118
  key qualities of 10–18
  for life coaches 92, 176
  acknowledging mistakes by
      116–8
  nurturing of 91–2
  professional issues for 159–76
  questions from 201–4
  sharing by 84–6
  specialty areas of 115–6
  teams of 194
  as traders in miracles 3
  unresolved problems of 113–5,
      198–9
  see also sessions
life coaching
  balance in the relationship and
      90–2
  benefits of 4–10, 176, 178, 179,
      182, 186
  as career 3, 19–21
  clients creating value from
      132
  commitment to clients and 5, 8,
      10, 28, 30
  cost of 25, 28, 186, 191-2,
      193–4
  as elitist field 193–4
  ending the relationship within
      43–6, 102, 172
  marketing for 44, 116, 177–92
  mechanics of 23–46
  power and possibility of 1–21
  qualifications for 184–5
  questions and answers about
      193–204
  stopping in certain areas 101–2
  of two people at once 108–12

  in unknown subject areas
      113–5
  verbal calling card for 180–2
  see also sessions
life plan 122
life survey 29–30, 154
life-coaching agreements 26–7,
      28, 169, 170, 173
life-coaching continuum 47–68
  adding to client's list of
      possibilities 47
  asking client to generate a few
      possibilities 47
  asking client to generate many
      possibilities 47
  listening fully and affirming
      47, 105–6, 108
  listening fully and feeding back
      problem 57, 89
  non-coaching techniques
      giving advice 61
      giving advice by sharing or
        questioning 64
      giving the answer 65
  offering an option 47
  presenting ten possibilities 47
  presenting three possibilities
      47, 59–60
  teaching a new technique 47
limitations of clients 2
listening 37
  active 54–5
  body and 49
  fully (power process) 155
  fully and affirming (coaching
      continuum) 48, 53, 105
  locus of control, external and
      internal 61

magic lantern 74
making and keeping promises
      (power process) 155
managed care 21
managing your associations
      (power process) 156

managing your interpretations
(power process)   155
marketing   44, 116, 177–92
  clarity in   177–8
  potential clients and   178, 179
  specialty areas and   115–6
  word-of-mouth   178
marriage   73, 144
Max, Peter   17–18
mechanics of life coaching   23–46
media in marketing   179–80
medication, psychiatric   169–70
meditation   18, 24, 53, 96, 98, 107, 127
mental disorders   20, 27, 165, 167, 169
  *see also Diagnostic and Statistical
  Manual of Mental Disorders*
mental health days   175
mental health professionals   27, 44, 167
mental space   52-3
microcredit   149
"might"   106
mind clearing   87
ministry   1
miracles   3, 11, 12, 53, 151, 159
mistakes   13, 54, 118
  acknowledging   116–8
  appreciating   155
  celebrating   118, 185
  by coaches   176
  forgiving   86
moment-to-moment choices   9, 36, 124, 154, 156
money   7, 19, 74, 193, 198
  see also fees for life coaching
mood changes   138
Murchison, Robbie   41
music   24, 53, 98, 181
Myers-Briggs Personality Profile   30

nature settings   98
non-acceptance   51–2

non-directive techniques   61, 92
nonverbal cues   80–1
notes   39–41
  by clients   121
  confidentiality of   32
  presentation of, to client   39–40
  reviewing   17, 32
  see also writing
noticing your expectations (power
process)   155
obligation, language of   106–7, 146
observations versus interpretations   142, 147
offering an option (coaching
continuum)   82
office assistant   189
Oh, God (movie)   126
older adults   184
options, *see* possibilities
"or" versus "and"   123
organizations, coaching for
employees in   186
oxygen as natural drug   53

passion   52, 106, 132, 185
  discovering   1–4, 20, 48, 69–77, 105
passions   75, 76, 105, 106
  brainstorming   74
  dreams and   75
  following   132
  questions about   74
past   20, 126, 127
  exploring   94
  releasing   86
  reviewing   76
patterns   87
persistence (power process)   155
personal growth and development   10, 154, 185
personal transformation   1, 3, 90, 154
personality types   136
physicians   166, 172

planning 106
possibilities
  client-generated 55–7, 111, 115,
    135, 179, 196
  adding to client's list of 57
  language of 106
  modeling 196
  choosing from 197
  coach-generated 57–60
  of life coaching 1–21
  expanded 5–6
potential clients 178, 179, 180,
    182, 184, 185, 194
poverty 149, 151
power processes 154, 200
  summary of 154–6
power
  imbalance in 164
  of life coaching 1–21
practicing acceptance (power
    process) 154
practicing without reproach 139
praying 96, 126, 135, 175
predicting the future 127
preference
  language of 106
  versus attachment 142–5
present 20, 85, 94
  focus on 126–7
"presenting issue" 20
presenting ten possibilities
    (coaching continuum) 57–9
presenting three possibilities
    (coaching continuum)
    59–60
priority setting 74, 130–1, 132,
    203
problems
  as habits 136–40
  solving 4, 60, 86, 120, 125,
    134–6
  specific 20
process versus content 102,
    153–4, 185, 200
professional associations 173

professional development 174–6,
    185, 190, 193
professional issues for life coaches
    159–76
promising 7, 13, 106, 155, 170
promotional materials 179–80
provocative therapy 199
psychiatrists 20, 167
psychoanalysis 20
psychotherapists 164, 172

questions 55, 71
  about life coaching 186–7,
    193–204
  about passions 74
  advice and 64–5
  caution with 92–5
  emotional release and 141
  into statements 58, 93–4
  as requests for evaluation 83
  too many 141
  what-if 73–4

race 18
racism 51–2
raising the stakes 120
Rapid City Journal 145
recreating the experience of
    another person 149–51
recreational activities 132
referrals 166–71
relationships
  balance in 90–2
  building 28
  defining new roles in 46
  dual 163–6
  ending 43–6
  improving 149–53
  long-term 30
  short-term 21, 25
  see also clients; life coaches;
    sessions
relaxation exercises 60
religious beliefs 125
Renaud, Michel 17, 18

Rentz, Bill   41
rescheduling   120
resignation in clients   196–7
revising your habits (power
    process)   155
rituals   45, 98–100
Rogers, Carl   47
role-playing   112, 196

sabbaticals   134, 175
sadness   136, 140–1, 148
safe physical and psychological
    environments   141
secretary   189
self-discipline   9–10, 139
self-disclosure   50
self-discovery   61
self-employment   185, 187–92
self-esteem   11, 136, 137, 139
self-evaluation   81–3
self-limitations   74
self-responsibility   105–8
    speaking with   146–9
self-selection of clients   182
sessions
    between   7–8, 23, 32, 33, 42
    canceling   195
    first   28–31, 173
    flexibility during   23
    focus during   36–9
    preparation for   33–5
    reviewing and previewing   32,
        42
    times and ways to meet   23–6
    see also clients; life coaches; life
        coaching; relationships
sexual attraction and clients
    161–3
sexual harassment   162
sexual preference   18
shame   7
sharing   84–6
    and advice   61
    by coaches   80
short-term coaching   21, 25

"shoulding"   6
skills of life coaching   69–118
social workers   20
solutions, brainstorming for   134
speaking candidly (power process)
    155
speaking dreams   121–2
speaking with self-responsibility
    146–9
specialty areas of life coaches
    115–6
spiritual paths   97
spiritual practices   127
spontaneity
    in coaching relationship   33, 75,
        95
    versus goal setting   123–5
stage fright   199–200
state laws   172
statements from questions   58,
    93–4
strengths and special interests of
    clients   132–4
strong vocational interest
    inventory   30
"stuck" clients   195–7
"stuffing" feelings   146
success strategies   153–7
success, celebrations of   86, 99
successful nature of clients   2
suffering   9–10, 139, 143
suicide   117, 187
support groups   63
surrender and trust (power
    process)   155
surveying your life (power
    process)   154
surveys and assessments   20,
    29–30
symbols   99, 110, 190

t'ai chi   98–9, 197
taping
    for debriefing   80
    of sessions   80

teaching   59, 60
  a new technique (coaching
    continuum)   60
  topics for   119–57
teams of life coaches   194
telephone, coaching by   23
therapy   94, 103–4, 169
  life coaching and   20–1, 103,
    168, 170
  provocative   199
thinking clearly (power process)
  155
threats   102
thwarted plans   76–7
touching 159, 162, 204
traveling, coaching while   26
triads   25
trust   155, 176, 194
two-week planning   129–32

unconditional acceptance as
    benefit of life coaching   7
unconditional love   103
unconditional positive regard   142
unethical activities   171–4
universal mind   97

vacations   175
  coaching during   16
value of life coaching   4, 6, 12,
  166, 178, 180
values   8, 15, 16, 28, 156
  conflicts between behaviors and
    30
venting feelings, *see* emotional
    discharge
verbal calling card,   180–2

verbal cues   45–6, 80–1
victimhood   103, 105
videotaping   80
vision as benefit of life coaching
  4–5
visualization   60, 135

walking   24, 45, 53, 92, 189, 197
"what" versus "how"   126, 128
"why?" questions   94-5
withheld information   111–2
word-of-mouth advertising
    178
  see also marketing
words
  habit of   107
  value of   40
working hours   189
workshops   175
world-class contribution   187
worrying about the future   127
worst possible event   145
writing   188
  action plans   38
  of agendas   53
  coaching with   24, 42
  on passions   74
  see also letters, coaching with;
    notes
written agreement   26–7, 28, 169,
    170, 173

yoga   197
you-messages   146, 149
Yunus, Muhammad   149

"zone", in the   33